Grandma's German Cookbook

Birgit Hamm
Linn Schmidt

Grandma's German Cookbook

More please!

"Stuffed peppers! I was twelve the last time I ate them!" In a small lunch bistro in Hamburg's Ottensen district, everyone is happy that today, alongside pasta with arugula pesto and chickpea curry, the chef has put something so exotic on the menu. The stuffed peppers sell out in minutes—after all, they aren't something you get every day! Whether it's stuffed peppers, cheese spätzle, or crêpes with strawberry jam, each one of us remembers a very special dish that takes us on a trip down memory lane, a very special dish that conjures up the carefree days of childhood and brings them alive. The memory of endlessly-long summer vacations when the sun shone every day, of being ravenous after coming out of the pool, of the hamburgers! Or when homemade chocolate pudding was served as a special treat after lunch.

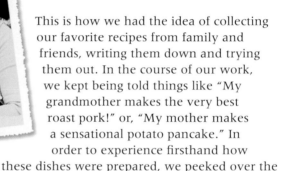

This is how we had the idea of collecting our favorite recipes from family and friends, writing them down and trying them out. In the course of our work, we kept being told things like "My grandmother makes the very best roast pork!" or, "My mother makes a sensational potato pancake." In order to experience firsthand how these dishes were prepared, we peeked over the shoulders of a number of grandmothers and diligently wrote down the recipes as they cooked their special dishes. They didn't only reveal their best dishes, but also recounted many interesting stories from their own lives.

We were especially impressed by the creativity and speed with which they cooked. Take a piece of butter, a bit of flour, and sugar and—presto—the streusel is made, and all without weighing a thing. "I cook by instinct," we often heard—but routine and skill are prerequisites for cooking by instinct. So of course we were eager to know the precise quantities of everything— how much butter really is used in the batter? At each step, we practically jumped in with the kitchen scales.

The fruit of our labors is a wide-ranging recipe collection—to bring back memories, to cook by, and, we hope, to allow you to enjoy dishes that, even in a small way, will awaken in you a few childhood memories—for example, of seemingly endless summer vacations.

Contents

Soups & Stews

Soljanka

To my friend Daniela, who grew up in Leipzig, Soljanka is a dish that fills her with nostalgia more than any other. Although it was very popular even in the former DDR, its belittlers insist that this tart, piquant, soup, of which there are countless versions, is made out of kitchen scraps. I don't know where its detractors tasted the dish, but they really should try Daniela's mother's version. Birgit

Serves 4–6

10½oz (300g) luncheon meat in thick slices

7oz (200g) kielbasa

2 cups onions

1 tbsp unsalted butter

4 red bell peppers

2 tomatoes

⅓ cup water

1 tsp mustard seeds

1 tsp caraway seeds

1 tsp cayenne pepper

1 tbsp sweet Hungarian paprika

5 allspice berries

2 bay leaves

1 tbsp tomato paste

1 tsp sugar

5½oz (150g) gherkins

3½fl oz (100ml) gherkin brine

2 cups vegetable or chicken broth

juice of 1 lemon

salt to taste

10½oz (300g) sour cream

Cut the luncheon meat and kielbasa into small cubes. Peel and dice the onions. Wash the red peppers and tomatoes. Remove the stems and seeds from the red peppers and cut into long, thin strips. Dice the tomatoes, keeping the juice. Melt the butter in a pot, add the sausage cubes and brown quickly. Add the onions and fry on high until nicely browned. Reduce the heat to medium and add the red peppers. Sauté for about 3 minutes. Add the tomatoes, their juice, and the water, and stir constantly to incorporate into the liquid the brown crust on the bottom. Reduce the heat to low. Add the mustard, caraway seeds, cayenne pepper, sweet paprika, allspice, bay leaves, tomato paste and sugar, stir, cover the pot and simmer gently.

Chop the gherkins finely and add them to the soup along with the gherkin brine. Pour in the broth, and bring it to a quick boil. Cover the pot, reduce the heat, and simmer over low heat for about 45 minutes, stirring now and then. Just before serving, add lemon juice and salt to taste. Place a dollop of sour cream on each plate of soup and serve.

Recipe photo on page 6

TIP Make two portions at the same time; Soljanka tastes even better when it is reheated. It also freezes well and is a great soup to serve at parties.

Chicken Soup

Whenever somebody in our family had a cold, our grandmother would make a hearty chicken soup—this was the best medicine, she insisted. And she was right. Since then, what people knew through experience has been proven to be correct by science: certain ingredients in chicken broth inhibit inflammation in the nose and throat. There is no reason, however, to wait for your next cold before making this delicious and nutritious soup. Birgit

Serves 6–8

1 large onion, unpeeled
¼ cup celery root
¼ cup carrots
3oz (90g) leek
4 sprigs of flat-leaf parsley
1 stewing chicken (or 2.2lb/1kg chicken backs or chicken thighs)
1 heaping tsp salt
5 peppercorns
5½oz (150g) soup noodles (alphabet noodles or stars)
3½oz (100g) peas (fresh or frozen)
2 tbsp chopped flat-leaf parsley

Cut the onion in half and place cut side down in a large pot. Put the pot on the stove and brown the onion halves at a high heat—this will give the soup a lovely deep golden-brown color. Clean and trim the celery root, carrots, leek, and parsley and chop into large pieces. Add 8½ cups cold water to the pot. Add the chicken, celery root, carrots, leek, parsley, salt, and peppercorns and bring everything to a boil. Reduce the heat to its lowest point and gently simmer the soup uncovered for 2 hours. Now and then, skim off any scum that rises to the surface.

Boil the soup noodles in salt water according to the instructions on the package. When the soup is cooked, remove the largest pieces of chicken and vegetables from the broth and set aside. Pour the broth through a fine sieve into another pot. If the soup is going to be eaten right away, skim off some of the fat from the surface of the liquid. Remove the chicken meat from the bone, tear it into pieces, and finely dice the carrot and celery root. Add the carrots, celery root, peas, and noodles to the soup and reheat briefly. Spoon into soup dishes, garnish each portion with parsley, and serve.

Recipe photo on page 7

TIP Chicken soup can easily be cooked in advance and it also freezes well. It is easier to remove the solidified chicken fat once the soup has cooled down in the refrigerator.
By substituting rice for the noodles, you can make a tasty chicken-and-rice soup. In a bowl, beat one egg per serving and pour the egg over a fork into the hot soup. Stir briefly and serve.

Wedding Soup

When my grandmother married, traditional Wedding Soup was, of course, part of the meal. This hearty chicken soup comes with a variety of garnishes that differ widely from region to region; however, they are always delicious. An extra pinch of salt is supposed to ensure healthy children. And, according to tradition, the first of the bride-pair to dip a spoon into the soup will be the boss in the marriage.   Birgit

Serves 8

For the omelet:
4 large eggs
½ cup milk
salt and pepper to taste
some freshly grated nutmeg
1 tsp softened unsalted butter

The vegetables:
2 carrots
½ cauliflower
4 asparagus stems
1 tsp salt

For the meatballs:
10½oz (300g) ground pork
salt and pepper to taste
1 onion
1 tbsp bread crumbs
1 medium egg

For the soup:
8½ cups chicken soup (page 9)
1 bunch of chives
3½oz (100g) cooked soup noodles

To make the omelet, beat the eggs and the milk and season with salt, pepper, and nutmeg. Preheat the oven to 275 °F (135 °C) or 250 °F (120 °C) on the convection setting. Butter a flat, ovenproof dish and pour in the egg mixture. Place the dish in a large pan and fill the pan with hot water so that the water comes up to ¾in (2cm) below the edge of the dish. Place the pan on the middle rack of the oven and bake the egg mixture for about 30 minutes until it sets. When it is set, remove the omelet and let cool. Cut into ⅓in (1cm) squares. Set aside.

To prepare the vegetable garnish, wash and peel the carrots and slice thinly. Wash and trim the cauliflower and separate into small florets. Peel the asparagus and cut into 1-in (3-cm) lengths. Bring a large pot of water to a boil, add the salt, and cook the vegetables until firm. Drain and shock with ice water.

To make the meatballs, place the ground pork in a bowl and season with salt and pepper. Mince the onions. Add the onions, bread crumbs and egg to the ground pork and mix thoroughly. Set it aside.

Bring the chicken soup to a boil and reduce the heat. Shape the ground pork into small meatballs. Add the meatballs to the soup and let simmer gently for about 5 minutes until they are cooked. Wash the chives and chop them very finely. Add the omelet, vegetables, and noodles to the soup until they are warmed through—about 3 minutes. Garnish with the chives.

Graubünden Barley Soup

As a child, my friend Martin spent his summer vacations on a small farm in the Swiss Canton of Graubünden. One day, during a hike, he and his family were caught unprepared by a thunderstorm. By the time they returned to the farmhouse, they were soaked through and shivering with cold. Fortunately, the farmer's wife had planned ahead and prepared a hearty, savory, barley soup for her guests that evening — and no-one came down with a cold.   Linn

Serves 4

1 small onion
1 leek
1 small carrot
1 small piece of Savoy cabbage
1 small piece of celery root
1oz (25g) air-dried beef such as bündnerfleisch or Bresaola
1 slice of uncooked ham (or smoked bacon)
1 tbsp unsalted butter
¼ cup barley
6⅓ cups vegetable, beef, or chicken broth
½ cup cream
salt to taste
coarsely-ground black pepper
freshly grated nutmeg
1 bunch of chives
whipped cream to taste

Peel the onion; wash, trim, and finely chop the leek, carrot, Savoy cabbage, and celery root. Cut the bündnerfleisch and raw ham into small cubes. Melt the butter in a large pot and add the vegetables, bündnerfleisch, ham, and barley, and sauté for about 5 minutes until the onion is translucent. Add the broth, bring it to a boil, and reduce the heat. Cover the pot and simmer gently for 1½ hours, or until the barley is cooked.

Stir the cream into the barley soup and season it with salt, pepper, and nutmeg. Return the soup to a boil and turn off the heat. Wash the chives and chop them very finely. Ladle out the soup into four bowls, and garnish with chives and whipped cream.

TIP Always freshly prepare this soup since barley swells up after it has sat for a few hours in the liquid and the soup becomes lumpy.

Crêpe Soup

Crêpe soup is known as "Flädlesuppe" in Swabia, where crêpes are known as "Flädle." They are rolled-up, cut into thin strips, and then placed in a clear savory broth. Traditionally, this soup was a typical way of using up leftovers. When beef or vegetable broth was left over from the previous day, it was easy (and quick) to make a few crêpes, cut them up finely, and serve them with the broth, making a delicious soup. This dish makes a wonderful light lunch or first course.

Serves 4

3½oz (100g) flour
2 large eggs
1⅓ cup (300ml) milk
1 pinch of salt
1 pinch of freshly grated nutmeg
2 tbsp clarified unsalted butter or vegetable oil
1 bunch of chives
about 4 cups broth to taste (such as the beef broth on page 25, or the vegetable broth on page 19)
pepper to taste

To make the pancakes, using a whisk, mix the flour, eggs, milk, and a generous pinch of salt and nutmeg in a bowl until the batter is no longer lumpy. Let the batter stand for 15 minutes. Melt the clarified butter or vegetable oil in a nonstick frying pan. Using a soup ladle, pour just enough batter into the frying pan to thinly cover the bottom. One after another, fry 3–4 thin pancakes. Let the pancakes cool slightly.

Roll up the pancakes tightly and slice them into thin rounds. Evenly divide the pancake rolls between four soup plates. Wash the chives and chop them very finely. Heat the broth, season to taste with salt and pepper, pour it over the pancakes, and garnish with a sprinkling of chives. Serve immediately.

TIP Pancake soup also tastes delicious garnished with wild garlic scapes, parsley, or other fresh herbs.

Green Bean, Pear, and Bacon Stew

Green beans with pears—is it possible that this combination could only have been invented by the good citizens of Hamburg? Yes, it's true. However, Hamburgers don't use large, sweet, pears such as Bartlett pears for this delicious stew, but small, hard, tart, cooking pears such as Seckel pears. Tart pears complement this savory stew superbly! You can also use other types of firm pears.   Linn

Serves 4

2 onions
1lb 2oz (500g) smoked bacon in one piece
5¼ cups water
2.2lb (1kg) green beans
1 bunch of savory
4 firm, tart, cooking pears, such as Seckels
salt and pepper to taste

Peel and quarter the onions. Place them and the bacon in a heavy-bottomed pot, add 5¼ cups water, and bring to a boil. Reduce the heat and cook gently for 30 minutes. In the meantime, wash and clean the green beans and cut them into bite-sized pieces. Add the green beans to the bacon and simmer for 15 minutes.

Wash the savory. Either pluck the leaves from the stems or bind the whole bunch with kitchen twine. Add the savory to the pot. Wash the pears and place them whole on top of the green beans and let them cook with the beans for another 10–15 minutes. When everything is cooked, season to taste with salt and pepper. Before serving, fish out the bacon and cut it into slices.

TIP This stew tastes great on its own, or you can serve it with rotini pasta or russet potatoes. To make a vegetarian version, substitute 9oz (250g) smoked tofu for the bacon. First, though, cook the onions for 10 minutes in vegetable broth, then proceed as described above. Before serving, cut the tofu into cubes, fry them in a bit of oil, and gently stir the tofu into the stew.

TIP If savory is not readily available in your area, you can substitute fresh thyme. Just reduce the quantity by half.

Vegetable Soup with Semolina Dumplings

This strictly vegetarian soup was served at my friend Marion's house each Thursday before Easter. In Catholic parts of Germany, it is customary to eat a meatless dish on this day. Surprisingly, the soup is solely vegetable-based. Not even a vegetable-broth cube adulterates the ingredients. If the soup sounds bland, it certainly doesn't taste it! Birgit

Serves 4

For the vegetable broth:

¼ celery root
1 large onion
2 large carrots
2 stalks of celery
2 tbsp unsalted butter
½ bunch of flat-leaf parsley
1 tsp tomato paste
1 level tsp salt
1 clove
¼ cup peas (fresh or frozen)
¼ cup chives chopped very finely

For the semolina dumplings:

½ cup milk
1 tbsp unsalted butter
salt to taste
1 large pinch of freshly-grated nutmeg
⅓ cup semolina
1 large egg

To make the soup, clean the celery root, onion, carrots, and celery, dice finely, melt the butter in a large pot, and sauté the vegetables. Chop the parsley and add it to the pot along with the tomato paste, salt, and the clove, stir, and sauté briefly with the vegetables. Pour 5¼ cups of cold water into the pot. Bring all the ingredients to a boil and simmer on a low heat for about 30 minutes, stirring every now and then. If scum rises to the surface, skim it off with a slotted spoon. During the last 5 minutes of the cooking time, add the peas and taste the soup again for seasoning. Add salt if needed.

To make the semolina dumplings, place the milk, butter, salt, and nutmeg in a small pot, bring to a boil, and remove from the heat. Add the semolina and cook, stirring constantly with a spoon, until a smooth ball forms and comes away from the sides of the pot. Then, beat in the egg. Using two teaspoons dipped into cold water now and then, cut out small dumplings from the semolina mixture. Place them directly into the simmering vegetable soup and let them poach in the liquid for 5 minutes. Ladle the soup and the dumplings into soup bowls and garnish with a sprinkling of chives.

TIP This soup also tastes very good as a noodle soup and is quickly made. Instead of semolina dumplings, add a handful of star noodles to the soup during the last 5 minutes of cooking time.

19

Green Pea Soup

This soup tastes wintry and hearty and yet, at the same time, agreeably light. Its secret: green split peas. These are dried, halved green peas—without the thick outer skin that give standard pea soup its grayish color and makes it hard to digest.

Serves 4

9oz (250g) dried green split peas
¼ cup celery root
¼ cup carrots
3oz (90g) leek
4 sprigs of flat-leaf parsley
1 tbsp unsalted butter or pork lard
1lb 2 oz (500g) smoked pork belly in one piece
4 medium yellow potatoes, such as Yukon Gold
3½oz (100g) frozen peas
1 tbsp fresh marjoram leaves
1 tsp salt
pepper to taste

Wash the split peas thoroughly and soak in about 6 cups of cold water for at least 2 hours. Clean and trim the celery root, carrots, leek, and parsley and chop into small pieces. In a large pot, melt the butter or pork lard and sweat the vegetables over a brisk heat. Add the parsley and the peas along with the soaking water and the piece of pork belly. Turn the heat up high and bring the soup to a boil. Skim the scum that rises to the surface of the liquid. Reduce the heat and, with the pan partially covered, gently simmer the soup for 30 minutes.

Peel the potatoes and cut them into small cubes. Add the potato cubes to the pot and cook the soup for another 30 minutes. Ten minutes before the end of the cooking time, add the frozen peas to the liquid.

Remove the pork belly from the pot and slice it into bite-sized pieces. Return the pork cubes to the soup, add the marjoram, and let steep for 2 minutes. Season the soup liberally with salt and pepper.

TIP If you like your soup a bit creamier, after you have removed the pork belly from the pot, use a hand-held blender to purée the peas until the soup has the consistency you like.

Emilie Frohn from the Rhineland

Dinner is ready!

Emilie Frohn still lives in her lovingly-decorated parents' house in the small wine-growing town of Engelstadt in Rhineland-Palatinate. Her property has a large garden, courtyard, barn, and a former cow stall, which, with its seven arches, resembles a small cathedral. Behind the house, fields and vineyards stretch all the way to the horizon. Steps away is the winery belonging to the Hoch family—close relatives of Emilie's—and it is practically her second home. Formerly, Emilie often conjured up meals for large numbers of people in the winery household: "Having visitors in the house was pretty much the norm," she recalls.

She has made one of her classic recipes for us, *Beef Soup with Marrow Dumplings*. At a typical Rhineland Sunday dinner, this soup is usually served as the first course. For Emilie, cooking means fun and routine at the same time: "Especially in fall, when friends and relatives come to help with the wine harvest, twenty people can crowd around the table in no time," she tell us. "The fall festival, which we celebrated every year after the grape harvest with all the helpers, was especially lovely."

On the one hand, Emilie is firmly rooted here, on the other, she always longed to travel to far-off countries: "I've seen a little bit of the world. I was in Brazil, in Chile, China … this was a while ago—but I really enjoyed it!" There was also a lot to discover from a culinary point of view on her travels. "I tried everything, even the most unusual things. The fact that everything always agreed with me lies in my positive attitude," explains Emilie, and adds, laughingly, "And a little schnapps after dinner—this helps, too."

Beef Soup with Marrow Dumplings

A Sunday dinner was unthinkable without soup, which was always the first course. Usually, the soup was a strong, clear broth that didn't fill you up, just gently prepared your stomach for the main course—like my godmother Emilie's "Beef Soup with Marrow Dumplings." And the best part is that the meat used to make the broth was served as the main course along with several tasty side dishes. Birgit

Emilie Frohn from the Rhineland

Serves 6

For the beef broth:

⅛ celery root

2 carrots

1 small onion

1 leek

2.2lb (1kg) soup bones

1 tsp granulated
beef broth or 1 beef
bouillon cube

3.3lb (1½kg) beef
(chuck or shoulder)

1 small sprig of lovage

1 tsp salt

pepper to taste

freshly grated nutmeg

*For the marrow
dumplings:*

1½oz (40g) beef marrow
(from 1–2 marrow bones)

1½oz (40g) softened
unsalted butter

1 tbsp finely chopped
flat-leaf parsley

1 extra-large egg

2–3oz (60–85g) bread
crumbs

salt to taste

freshly grated nutmeg

6⅓ cups water

To make the broth, clean the celery root, carrots, onion, and leek. Place the soup bones and the granulated broth or bouillon cube in a large pot, add 10½ cups cold water, and bring to a boil. When the water has boiled, add the beef, celery root, carrots, and onion. Reduce the heat to low and cover the pot with a lid. Let the broth simmer gently, keeping the lid closed. Now and then, skim off any scum that rises to the surface of the liquid. After the broth has cooked for about 1 hour, add the leek and lovage. Let the soup simmer for 1 hour more.

Remove the meat, pour the soup through a fine sieve, and return the liquid to the pot. Turn off the heat. Season the broth liberally with salt, pepper, and nutmeg. If desired, finely chop the carrots and celery root and add them as a garnish to the soup. Keep the soup warm.

To make the marrow dumplings, remove the marrow from the bones, mash with a fork, and beat until slightly frothy. Add the butter, parsley, egg, and bread crumbs and combine everything thoroughly. Season with the salt and nutmeg and put the mixture in the refrigerator, uncovered, to rest for 1–2 hours.

In a large pot, bring 6⅓ cups salted water to a boil and reduce the heat to its lowest point. Flour your hands and make a small test dumpling. Add the test dumpling to the barely simmering water. If the dumpling breaks apart, stir more bread crumbs into the dumpling mixture. Then, re-flour your hands, shape about 18 dumplings, and poach them in barely-simmering water for 20 minutes—do not cook them longer. Place the dumplings in a soup terrine or on individual soup plates and pour the hot beef broth over them.

TIP If the main course is going to be *Beef with Horseradish Sauce* (*see* page 97), return the cooked beef to the broth until it is needed so that it will keep warm and not dry out.

The marrow bones can be frozen with a bit of the broth. They will yield one more good soup base for a second meal.

Potato Soup

Potato soup has to be my absolute favorite soup. We had it every Monday for dinner garnished with a lot of parsley fresh from the garden. This isn't an elegant Sunday dinner soup, but a thick and creamy soup that is ideal for Mondays!   Linn

Serves 4–6

1¾lb (800g) white potatoes, such as russet potatoes
1 large carrot
1 leek
3½oz (100g) celery root
1 medium onion
1 tbsp unsalted butter
5¼ cups vegetable broth
salt to taste
white pepper
2 tsp chopped marjoram (fresh or dried)
⅓ cup heavy cream
1 tsp mustard
4 hot dogs
1 bunch of flat-leaf parsley

Wash the potatoes, carrot, leek, and celery root and dice them finely. Peel the onion and dice it finely. Melt the butter in a pot and sauté the onion until it is translucent. Add the diced vegetables and cook them for 1–2 minutes. Then, stir in the vegetable broth. Bring the broth to a boil and let it simmer over moderate heat for about 30 minutes.

Using a potato masher, mash the cooked vegetables in a pot and season them to taste with the salt, white pepper, and marjoram. Mix in the heavy cream and the mustard. Then purée the soup with a hand-held blender and taste for seasoning once again. Cut the hot dogs into pieces and warm them up in the soup. Pluck the parsley leaves from the stems and chop them finely. Ladle the soup into soup bowls and garnish with the chopped parsley.

TIP For an even heartier taste, add parsnips or turnips to the vegetable mix and substitute cooked sausage, such as kielbasa, for the hot dogs. The soup is also delicious when you use a mixture of half sweet potatoes and half white potatoes.

Hamburg Shrimp Soup

North Sea shrimp are the main ingredient in this excellent soup; however, if they are not readily available, you can use small North Atlantic shrimp instead. In the past, a stock made from the shells of the tiny North Sea shrimp were used for the soup base. But unpeeled North Sea or North Atlantic shrimp are hard to come by. Instead, just use shellfish (or fish) stock for the soup base to make this flavorful, creamy, soup! Birgit

Serves 4–6

¼ cup celery root
¼ cup carrots
3oz leek
4 sprigs of flat-leaf parsley
4¼ cups shellfish stock (alternatively, fish stock)
1 cup dry white wine
½ tsp salt
1 pinch of saffron threads
1 bunch of dill
1 tsp tomato paste
1 pinch of sugar
1 cup heavy cream
¾lb (350g) cooked North Sea or North Atlantic shrimp, peeled and deveined

Clean and trim the celery root, carrots, leek, and parsley and chop into small pieces. Bring the shellfish or fish stock to a boil in a pot, add the vegetables, white wine, and salt, and cook over moderate heat until the vegetables are cooked through. Purée the soup in the pot using a hand-held blender.

While the soup is gently cooking away, ladle a bit of the cooking liquid into a small bowl and place the saffron threads in it to dissolve. Finely chop the dill. Stir half of the dill, the dissolved saffron, tomato paste, and sugar into the puréed soup. Reduce the heat and add ¾ cup of the heavy cream. Stir well and turn off the heat.

Set aside about 20 shrimp to use as a garnish later on. Add the remaining shrimp to the hot soup and gently warm the shrimp until they are just heated through; they must not boil. Taste the soup for seasoning and add more salt if needed. Whip the remaining heavy cream (¼ cup) until it forms stiff peaks. Ladle the soup into soup bowls and garnish each bowl with a dollop of whipped cream, the shrimp that were set aside, and the remaining chopped dill.

TIP If you don't have a hand-held blender, you can push the soup vegetables through a very fine sieve and then put them back in the soup. Adding 2 tablespoons of sweet sherry and a few drops of lemon juice to the soup gives it an extra lift.

Lentils with Spätzle

This Swabian national dish has perked me up on many a gray winter's day since, traditionally, one only eats this lentil dish between October and March. And too, this flavorful stew is one of those that tastes even better warmed up the next day.   Linn

Serves 4
1¾ cups brown lentils
10 cups cold water
1 bay leaf
2 medium onions
3½oz (100g) celery root
2 medium-sized carrots
3 tbsp vegetable oil
1 tbsp crushed mustard seed
2 cups beef, chicken, or vegetable broth
salt and pepper to taste
1 tbsp mustard
1 tbsp apple cider vinegar
4–8 hot dogs

Pick over the lentils, wash them, place them in a bowl, and cover them with cold water to soak, preferably overnight. The next day, pour the lentils into a sieve set over a large bowl to capture the soaking water. Pour 4¼ cups of the soaking water into a large pot and add the lentils and the bay leaf. Cover the pot and simmer the lentils for about 40 minutes over moderate heat until they are soft.

Peel the onions, celery root, and carrots and dice them finely. Heat the oil in a large pot, add the diced onions, and cook them until they are golden brown. Add the celery root, carrots, and the mustard seed to the pot and sauté. Pour in the broth, stir well, and simmer for 5 minutes. Then add the lentils with their remaining soaking water. Season with salt, pepper, and mustard. Turn the heat down to its lowest point and simmer the soup for another 15–20 minutes. Stir the lentils often since they tend to burn quickly. If there isn't enough liquid, add a bit more broth. Season the lentils with apple cider vinegar and add some more seasonings if needed. Once they are ready, add the pieces of hot dogs and gently warm them up.

TIP Traditionally, spätzle are served with lentils (*see* page 44 but leave out the cheese). Immediately after you have ladled out the lentils, add 1 tablespoon of apple cider vinegar to each bowl—the vinegar's tartness allows the flavor of the dish to fully unfold. For those who like a heartier version, add 3½oz (100g) of finely diced bacon to the onions as you are browning them.

Pichelsteiner Stew

As a child, I loved Mickey Mouse and Fix & Foxi comics and could spend hours and hours wrapped up in the many adventures of a Stone Age family called "The Pichelsteiners." I was convinced that "Pichelsteiner Stew," which we often ate at my grandmother's house on Saturdays, was the favorite dish of Neolith and Theolith, the two strong, but somewhat simple, brothers who lived in the Schachtelhalmwald. In truth, the hearty stew was served for the very first time in 1847 in the Bavarian Forest. And there is no mammoth meat in it. Even so, it still tastes delicious. Birgit

Serves 4

1lb 2oz (500g) yellow potatoes, such as Yukon Gold
2.2lb (1kg) mixed vegetables such as carrots, parsnips, leek, and Brussel sprouts
1 onion
9oz (250g) beef brisket
9oz (250g) pork shoulder, bones and skin removed
3½oz (100g) bacon
1 tbsp vegetable oil (as needed)
salt
1 tsp sweet Hungarian paprika
½ tsp caraway seeds
1 tbsp flat-leaf parsley
2 cups hot water

Wash and clean or peel the potatoes and vegetables and chop them up into even-sized pieces. Finely dice the onions. Cut the meat up into cubes about ¾in (2cm) in size. Slice the bacon into strips. Put the bacon into a pot without any fat in it and fry it at a high heat until all the fat has melted. Add the meat and onions to the fat—if needed, add 1 tablespoon of oil—and sauté over moderate heat until everything is golden-brown in color. Season with the salt and paprika. Cover the pot, reduce the heat to its lowest point, and simmer the stew for about 15 minutes, stirring often.

Arrange the potatoes and vegetables in layers on top of the meat. Season each layer with salt and caraway seeds. The final layer should be a layer of potatoes. Chop the parsley and sprinkle it over the stew. Slowly, so as not to disturb the layers, pour 2 cups of hot water down the inside of the pot. Do not stir! Cover with the lid and cook on the lowest heat for about 45 minutes. When the stew is cooked, gently stir the ingredients and serve immediately.

TIP Vary the vegetables according to the season: In summer, for example, you can use green beans instead of wintery Brussel sprouts. Savoy cabbage and green cabbage are also popular ingredients. No one vegetable should dominate the stew so make sure to select the types carefully. It is crucial to stir the stew just before serving and not earlier. In this way, none of the ingredients will fall apart and each layer will retain its unique flavor.

Everyday Meals

Stuffed Peppers

Peppers have to be filled with well seasoned ground meat. I can't stand the grass-colored things if they are cooked any other way; indeed, in the 1960s, it seemed that there were only green peppers to be had. Somehow, over the years, stuffed peppers have gone utterly out of fashion. When I recently brought a few in to work and warmed them up in the kitchen, the aroma attracted my colleagues in droves: "That smells really good!" — "What is it?" — "I haven't eaten this in ages! Can I please have the recipe?" Yes, certainly.... Birgit

Serves 4

4 red bell peppers
4 green bell peppers
1 onion
1¾lb (800g) mixed ground meat (pork, veal, beef)
2 tbsp finely chopped flat-leaf parsley
2 tbsp bread crumbs
2 large eggs
1 tsp salt
1 tsp sweet Hungarian paprika
½ tsp cayenne pepper
a pinch of pepper
1–2 cups hot broth to taste

Wash the peppers and cut a lid from the stem end of each one. Set the lids aside and remove the seeds and ribs. Slice the bottoms of the peppers slightly so that they stand upright on their own. Peel and finely dice the onion. Thoroughly combine the ground meat with the onion, parsley, bread crumbs, eggs, salt, paprika, cayenne pepper, and pepper. Preheat the oven to 375 °F (190 °C) or 350 °F (180 °C) on the convection setting.

Fill each pepper to the top with the ground meat mixture. Place the peppers in a suitable casserole dish and pour in enough broth so that the liquid comes up the sides of the peppers about ¾in (2cm). Set the casserole on the middle rack of the oven and cook for about 30 minutes. Then, place the lids on the peppers and cook for another 15 minutes. If needed, pour in a bit more broth so that the bottoms of the peppers do not stick to the casserole and burn. Place the peppers on plates and serve immediately.

Recipe photo on page 34

TIP Rice and tomato sauce go well with stuffed peppers, but the peppers also taste good just on their own. Making a vegetarian filling is a good way of using rice left over from the previous day. Instead of ground meat, combine cooked rice with peas, onions, parsley, and mushrooms sautéed in butter. Then, add the eggs and spices listed above and mix thoroughly. Place the mixture in the peppers, cook as above, and serve with tomato sauce.

Grandmother Dorothea's Pan-fried Potatoes

Pan-fried potatoes are one of those simple dishes that are extremely hard to make well. My grandmother's version were always perfect every time. Her fried potatoes were always the main attraction—so unrivaled, that all that they brooked as a side dish was a green salad. Her secret: no onions. And too, the potatoes absolutely had to be cooked the day before. After many more-or-less successful experiments—with onions, with bacon, with herbs and spices—I always returned to Grandmother Dorothea's fried potato recipe. It is simply second to none. Birgit

Serves 4

2.2lb (1kg) yellow potatoes, such as Yukon Gold
salt to taste
½ tsp caraway seeds
5–7 tbsp vegetable oil
a pinch of white pepper

The day before you plan on making this dish, wash the potatoes and place them in a large pot. Pour in enough water to barely cover the potatoes. Add the salt and the caraway seeds and bring the potatoes to a boil. Depending on the size of the potatoes, boil them for about 12–15 minutes until they are just cooked. They are done when the tip of a small sharp knife is easily inserted into the middle of a potato. Turn off the heat. Drain the potatoes, return them to the pot, place them on the burner you have just turned off, and shake the potatoes back and forth in the pot until all the water has evaporated. Remove the pot from the stove and let the potatoes cool for 5 minutes. Peel them immediately and then cover them with a dish towel and put them in the refrigerator until the next day.

Heat the oil in a large, heavy, frying pan. Cut the potatoes into ¼in (5mm) slices, place them in the hot oil, and fry over moderate heat. Do not stir the potatoes during the first 5 minutes. At most, you can shake the frying pan a bit so that the potatoes don't stick. Once the potatoes are golden-brown on one side, turn them over carefully using a spatula and a fork. If needed, add a bit more vegetable oil and continue frying until the slices are crispy brown all over. Season liberally with salt and pepper and serve immediately.

Recipe photo on page 35

TIP Never fry too many potato slices in the frying pan at one time or they won't become crispy. Ideally, fry the potatoes in several batches, or use two frying pans simultaneously, doubling the amount of vegetable oil. The potatoes turn out best in a cast-iron skillet or a heavy, nonstick frying pan.

Meat Patties Toni Style

My father Anton (known as Toni) enjoyed cooking as a form of relaxation. He was quite playful, and was always coming up with new ways of turning simple dishes into special ones, just like these meat patties. To make them, he cooked a piece of raw ham, put it through a meat grinder, added a small, dried, chile pepper, and mixed this into the ground meat. The result looks like a completely normal hamburger but it tastes much more flavorful. Birgit

Serves 4–6

6⅓ cups cold water
1 bay leaf
7oz (200g) raw country-style ham in one piece
1 day-old bread roll
½ cup milk
1 large onion
1 small, dried, chile pepper
1lb 2oz (500g) mixed ground meat (beef, pork, veal)
1 tsp salt
½ tsp pepper
1 extra-large egg
3 tbsp pork lard or clarified unsalted butter

Bring the water and the bay leaf to a boil in a pot. Place the ham in the water and boil over moderate heat for 1 hour. Remove the ham and let it cool down a bit. Then, using the coarsest disk of your meat grinder, grind the ham. Alternatively, using a large knife, dice the ham very finely.

Soak the bread roll in the milk and then squeeze out the milk. Finely dice the onion. Crumble up the chile pepper. In a bowl, thoroughly combine the ground meat with the ham, soaked bread, onion, chile pepper, salt, pepper, and egg. It is best if you use your hands for this. Then, moisten your hands and shape the ground meat mixture into 12 small patties.

Melt the pork lard or clarified butter in a large frying pan. Place the meat patties carefully in the fat and cook them over moderate heat for about 4–5 minutes on each side until they are golden-brown and crispy on the outside.

TIP These meat patties taste best just out of the frying pan, served with mashed potatoes and a vegetable such as kohlrabi. They also taste delicious cold, served with mustard and dill pickles as a party snack. For those who like classic hamburger patties best, leave out the chile pepper and replace the ham with 7oz (200g) ground meat.

Wiener Goulash

Whether it is know as "Szegediner Goulash with Sauerkraut," "Paprikás with Sour Cream," or "Pörkölt," with its thick, heavily reduced, sauce, this dish with Hungarian roots exists in untold variations. The goulash made in our family was a "Wiener Goulash," as my father was fond of emphasizing. For this version, equal parts of onions and meat are braised practically in their own juices. And even today, this is still my favorite kind of goulash. Birgit

Serves 4–6

2.2lb (1kg) boneless beef round

2.2lb (1kg) onions

1 clove of garlic

3 tbsp pork lard or clarified unsalted butter

2 heaping tbsp sweet Hungarian paprika

1 tbsp cayenne pepper

1 tsp tomato paste

1 tsp sugar

salt and pepper to taste

½ tsp ground caraway seeds

1 bay leaf

¼–⅓ cup red wine (or water)

Cut up the beef into cubes about 1½in (4cm) in size. Peel the onions and chop them coarsely. Either chop the garlic finely or grate it. In a heavy casserole that has a close-fitting lid, melt the butter or lard over high heat. Brown the cubes of beef in the fat on all sides until they are nicely browned. Add the onions and garlic to the beef and cook them until the onions have become lightly colored.

Reduce the heat. Sprinkle the meat and onions with the Hungarian paprika, stir, and cook everything over moderate heat for a few minutes. Add the tomato paste, sugar, salt, pepper, caraway seeds, and bay leaf and stir until everything is well combined. Reduce the heat, pour in ¼ cup red wine and stir. Immediately place the lid on the casserole. Turning the heat to its lowest point, braise the goulash on the stove for about 2 hours. Stir now and then and, if needed, add a bit of liquid. The cooked onions and the gelatin contained in the meat serve to slightly thicken the sauce.

TIP Wiener goulash is usually served with fresh, crusty, country-style bread cut into thick slices; however, short spiral pasta known as *rotini* and egg noodles also go well with goulash.

Red Herring Salad

My friend Jutta has a love-hate relationship with herring salad. To be more specific, first came the hate, then came the love. Jutta usually spent her summer vacations at her Grandmother Hermine's house. Hermine was a good woman through and through, but she insisted on serving herring salad five times a week. "Fish is good for the brain," she would always say. After two forkfuls, Jutta was stuffed — but afterwards, she secretly would devour a bar of chocolate. Today, she enjoys making her own herring salad using Grandmother Hermine's recipe — but only when her own children are not at home for dinner. Birgit

Serves 4–6

2 large eggs
1 red onion
½lb (225g) yellow potatoes, such as Yukon Gold, cooked in their skins the previous day
1 crisp tart apple
4 pickled herring filets (from a jar)
1 dill pickle
2 cooked red beets (from a can or jar)
4 tbsp mayonnaise
⅓ cup dill pickle liquid from the pickle jar
1 tsp sugar
½ tsp salt

Boil the eggs for 8–10 minutes until they are hard cooked, cool them in cold water, and peel them. Peel the onion and chop it finely. Core and peel the apple and peel the potatoes. Drain the herring. Chop the herring, apple, pickle, eggs, potatoes, and red beets into small pieces and place them in a bowl. Add the onion. In another bowl, make the herring salad dressing by combining the mayonnaise with the dill pickle liquid, sugar, and salt. Pour the dressing over the ingredients in the bowl, stir everything carefully, and cover the bowl. Let the herring salad marinate in the refrigerator for a day. Just before serving, stir the salad one more time.

TIP For a slightly different version of this salad, replace the red onion with 3 finely chopped scallions.

43

Cheese Spätzle

In my boyfriend's Swabian family, spätzle had to be cut by hand. As someone who comes from Northern Germany, I can only say the outcome is, for the inexperienced, a thick, lumpy, unappetizing mess. But, by using a spätzle maker, anyone can make this delicious Swabian specialty themselves in no time. It is worth buying a spätzle maker to make this recipe! Linn

Serves 4

4½ cups all-purpose flour
5 large eggs
¾–1 cup bottled sparkling water
1 tsp salt
10½–14oz (300–400g) grated Gruyere cheese
a pinch of pepper
4 onions
3 tbsp unsalted butter
3 stems flat-leaf parsley

Preheat the oven to 400°F (200°C). In a tall pot, bring about 12½ cups of well-salted water to a boil. Grease an ovenproof casserole dish. Sift the flour into a bowl and add the eggs. Using a rotary hand mixer, blend together the ingredients. Mix in the sparkling water a little bit at a time. Add the salt last. The dough should drip off a cooking spoon slowly. If it is too thick, add a bit more water; if it is too runny, add a bit more flour.

Ladle a portion of the dough into the spätzle maker and let the dough drop through into the boiling water. The spätzle are ready when they rise to the top, which only takes about 2–3 minutes. Skim the spätzle from the surface of the water with a slotted spoon, drain, and place them in the casserole. Sprinkle some of the cheese and pepper over each layer. Repeat these steps until you have used up all the dough and cheese. At the very end, sprinkle 1 tablespoon of the cooking water over the spätzle.

Place the cheese spätzle on the middle rack of the oven and bake them for 15 minutes. While they are baking, peel the onions and cut them into rings and clean and chop the parsley finely. Melt the butter in a frying pan and sauté the onion rings until they are golden brown. Remove the spätzle from the oven and place the onion rings on top. Garnish the spätzle with a bit of chopped parsley.

TIP Serving a leafy green salad with the spätzle is practically a must.

Schupf Noodles

These delicious little potato dumplings are known in Germany by various names. They are even called finger noodles, since they are finger-shaped. I first sampled schupf noodles at the Stuttgart Christmas Market, where they are served with sauerkraut. My friend Ilka entrusted me with her grandmother's recipe. She served them every Sunday with the roast and, during the week, with a green salad. Linn

Serves 4

1¾lb (800g) yellow potatoes, such as Yukon Gold

5½oz (150g) all-purpose flour

2 large eggs

1 tsp salt

1 pinch of freshly grated nutmeg

2 tbsp oil or clarified unsalted butter

Wash the potatoes in boiling water, boil them in their skins, and let them cool down completely. Then peel the potatoes and push them through a potato ricer into a bowl or mash them with a potato masher. Add the flour, eggs, salt, and nutmeg and, using your hands, knead the ingredients together until a dough forms. The dough should not be sticky to the touch. If needed, add a bit of flour or water to get the right consistency.

Shape the dough into a roll about 2in (5cm) in diameter. Slice the roll into pieces ⅓in (1cm) thick. Using your hands or a floured working surface, roll each piece back and forth until it forms a long roll that is pointed at each end. Repeat until all the dough is used up. Melt the 2 tablespoons of oil or clarified butter in a frying pan and cook the schupf noodles over moderate heat, turning often, until they are golden brown.

TIP Serve this dish with a leafy green salad, such as field greens or mâche. The quantities given in the recipe above are for a side dish. Schupf noodles can be prepared from potatoes left over from the previous day.

Mushroom Goulash with Bread Dumplings

This dish awakens childhood memories of hiking trips in Bavaria in the fall. Just like most children, I hated long hikes. It was only because every hour my father would hold out the promise of dumplings with mushroom stew— like a carrot and a stick— that I am not still sitting sulkily on a rock somewhere between the mountains and a lake.   Birgit

Serves 4

For the bread dumplings:

8 day-old bread rolls
1 cup milk
½ bunch of flat-leaf parsley
2 large eggs
salt, pepper, nutmeg to taste

For the goulash:

½ bunch of flat-leaf parsley
1 onion
1¾lb (800g) mixed mushrooms (such as white, chanterelle, cremini, portobello, king oyster, oyster, or shitake mushrooms)
2 tbsp unsalted butter
1 tsp fresh thyme leaves
½ cup dry white wine
1 cup heavy cream
1 pinch of sugar
salt to taste
a pinch of black pepper
a pinch of freshly grated nutmeg

To make the bread dumplings, cut the bread rolls into ⅓in (1cm) cubes and place them in a bowl. Warm the milk and pour it over the bread cubes. Let stand, covered, for 30 minutes. Wash the parsley, shake it dry, and chop it finely. Squeeze the bread well to remove excess liquid. Add the parsley and eggs, and combine well. Season liberally with salt, pepper, and nutmeg. In a large pot, bring well-salted water to a boil. Moisten your hands and shape 8–10 firm balls from the dough. Place the dumplings into the boiling water and return the water to a boil, immediately reduce the temperature and let the dumplings simmer for 20 minutes.

To make the goulash, wash the parsley, shake it dry, and chop it finely. Peel and mince the onion. Trim and clean the mushrooms. Cut the larger mushrooms into pieces. Melt the butter in a large, heavy, frying pan, sweat the onion, add the mushrooms, parsley, and thyme and sauté for about 5 minutes. Pour in the wine, stir well, and cook until all the wine has evaporated. Pour in the cream and, stirring constantly, cook for 2–3 minutes until the sauce has thickened. Season to taste with the sugar, salt, pepper, and nutmeg. Serve with bread dumplings.

TIP Mushrooms quickly absorb water and turn spongy when you wash them. Instead, thoroughly brush off any dirt using a mushroom brush. If you like, you can sprinkle parsley over the dish before serving.

Pan-Fried Fish with Potato Salad

Why was fish formerly usually eaten on Fridays? It was because, leaning on the Good Friday tradition, every Friday became a day of fasting, a day when you were not allowed to eat any meat if you were a good Catholic or even a good Protestant. Today, the rules are more relaxed. Even so, Fridays in our house were traditionally fish days. Hamburg-style potato salad filled with crisp pieces of apple converted even the Southern German side of my family into fans.   Linn

Serves 4

For the potato salad:

2.2lb (1kg) yellow potatoes, such as Yukon gold

salt to taste

1 large egg

4 dill pickles

1 large, tart apple, such as Granny Smith (about 200g)

9oz (250g) mayonnaise

½ tsp sweet Hungarian paprika

pepper

½ bunch of chives

For the pan-fried fish:

1¾lb (800g) fillets of fish, such as cod or haddock

juice of 1 lemon

salt to taste

2 tbsp flour

1 large egg

½ cup bread crumbs

5–8 tbsp vegetable oil

4 lemon slices, cut in half

To make the potato salad, wash the potatoes and cook them in their skins for about 20 minutes in boiling, salted, water. Drain, rinse them with cold water, and let them cool down a bit. Peel the potatoes and slice them into ¼in (5mm) pieces. Put the potatoes in a bowl. Cook the egg for 8–10 minutes until it is hard-boiled. Rinse the egg under cold water, peel it, dice it finely, and add it to the potatoes. Finely dice the dill pickles and add them to the bowl. Peel and dice the apple and add it to the salad. Add the mayonnaise. Stir everything carefully. Season with the cayenne pepper, salt, and pepper. Chop the chives finely and sprinkle them over the salad.

To make the pan-fried fish, wash the fish fillets, pat them dry, and cut them into pieces as desired (such as fish sticks). Sprinkle the fillets with lemon juice and salt. Set up a row of three plates to create a breading station. Place the flour on the first plate, the beaten egg on the second, and the bread crumbs on the third. Successively dip both sides of each piece of fish into the flour, beaten egg, and the bread crumbs, Press the pieces firmly into the bread crumbs. Heat the oil in a heavy-bottomed frying pan and, over moderate heat, fry the battered fish pieces for about 4 minutes on each side until they are crisp and golden-brown. Serve them on individual plates with a helping of potato salad. Garnish each plate with half a lemon slice.

TIP You can add grated coconut or chopped nuts to the bread crumbs.

Irma Spurzem from the Eifel

Tradition With a Modern Touch

All those who think of crocheted pot holders and filtered coffee when they hear the words "traditional German cooking" should drop by Irma Spurzem's apartment. Her designer kitchen is colored in rich-brown wood tones, the giant stainless-steel refrigerator sparkles, as does the glossy black work counter. The apartment is light and tastefully furnished in the minimalist style. Irma is comfortable in her trendy new condominium. Not long ago, she and her husband moved to the city, leaving behind a large house with a gorgeous view of the hilly landscape of the Vulkaneifel, near Koblenz. They moved because there is more going on in the city and their son and daughter-in-law live here. The couple often comes by for dinner now, and is happy to do so, partly because Irma's version of the original Rhineland "Sausage-and-Potato Casserole" is unmatched.

Even though the helpings are often quite rich, Irma Spurzem was once used to a very different scale of entertaining. Along with her husband, she was the head housekeeper of the North-Rhine-Westphalia State Government guesthouse in Bonn for 30 years. She regularly catered meals and receptions for 50 or more, and sometimes even garden parties for 5000. German political luminaries such as Johannes Rau, Joschka Fischer, Gerhard Schröder, and Helmut Schmidt, and international political figures and artists such as Henry Moore and Leonard Bernstein, all dined at Irma's table. And she has a story to tell about each one. "One could write scores of books about those times" she says. Knowing Irma, anything is possible.

Sausage-and-Potato Casserole

This typical Rhineland dish ("Döppekooche") is traditionally eaten in the fall. Irma Spurzem uses an old family recipe passed on to her by her mother to make her casserole. By adding quark or yogurt, the casserole turns out light and pale. No wonder Irma's son Karl swoons over it! The tip came from him and now we are also members of the non-profit "Eat More Sausage-and-Potato Casserole Society."

Serves 6–8

4¼ cups milk
6 day-old bread rolls
4½lb (2kg) yellow potatoes
2.2lb (1kg) onions
9oz (250g) bacon
6 large eggs
a pinch of black pepper
freshly grated nutmeg
salt to taste
1lb 2oz (500g) quark
(alternatively, use a thick
and creamy, plain, non-fat
yogurt)
½ cup vegetable oil
8 smoked sausages

Slightly warm the milk and add the bread to soak. Peel the potatoes and grate them finely. Peel the onions. Finely dice the onions and chop the bacon into small pieces. Combine the grated potatoes and the onions in a large mixing bowl. Stir in the eggs and liberally season the mixture with pepper, freshly grated nutmeg, and salt. Gently squeeze the bread and stir it and the quark or yogurt into the potato mixture. Combine everything thoroughly. Preheat the oven to 350°F (180°C) or 325°F (170°C) on the convection setting.

In a large ovenproof pot or heavy-bottomed roasting pan, sweat the bacon in the vegetable oil over moderate heat. Add the potato mixture to the bacon and stir thoroughly. Place the sausages in the mixture, poking them down so that they are completely covered. Smooth the top. Place the pot, uncovered, on the middle rack of the oven and bake for 2 hours. After about 1½ hours, check to make sure the crust is not getting too dark. If so, loosely cover the pot with aluminum foil.

Frankfurt Herb Sauce

Every Hessian family in and around Frankfurt—including my husband's—has its own special recipe for this divine sauce that even Goethe knew and loved. Most people do agree though that seven different herbs should be used. My husband's grandmother always put the herbs through the meat grinder to chop them as finely as possible. Her recipe is superb; however, I recommend using a kitchen machine.   Birgit

Serves 4

9 large eggs
1 bunch each of chives, flat-leaf parsley, borage, sorrel, salad burnet, chervil, and watercress
7oz (200g) crème fraîche
14oz (400g) sour cream
4½oz (125g) quark (alternatively, use a thick and creamy, plain, non-fat yogurt)
1 level tsp mustard
2 tsp salt
2.2lb (1kg) yellow potatoes, such as Yukon Gold
½ tsp caraway seeds
small pieces of butter for the potatoes

Cook the eggs for 8–10 minutes until they are hard-boiled. Peel the eggs. Chop 1 egg finely and set it aside. Wash the herbs, pat them dry, and chop them coarsely. Put the crème fraîche in the food processor, add the herbs, and purée. Gradually add the sour cream, quark or yogurt, mustard, and 1 level teaspoon salt to the food processor and mix thoroughly. The sauce should be thick and creamy. Place the sauce in a bowl and stir in the chopped egg. Taste for seasoning. Add a bit of salt if needed.

Scrub the potatoes and place them in a pot. Add 1 teaspoon of the salt and the caraway seeds. Fill the pot with cold water until the potatoes are just covered. Set the lid on the pot, bring the water to a boil, and cook the potatoes over moderate heat for about 20 minutes or until they are done. Turn off the heat. Drain the potatoes, return them to the pot, and shake them back and forth until all the water has evaporated. Peel the potatoes and keep warm.

To serve, place 1 large ladle of herb sauce onto each plate along with 2 hard-boiled eggs and a few peeled potatoes. Distribute the pieces of butter over the potatoes and salt to taste.

TIP If you don't have a food processor, or if you prefer hand-chopped herbs, chop the herbs very finely and stir them into the liquid with a large wire whisk. If you have trouble finding any of the herbs listed above, substitute baby field greens, arugula, lovage or stalk celery leaves, young beet leaves—whatever you like. Just keep in mind that no one herb should dominate.

Flottbeker Salad

Almost every day when I was a child I went to my friend Kirstin's house. Her grandmother lived in an apartment on the top floor. We often played dress-up, and would pay formal visits to Kirstin's grandmother clothed in gigantic hats and dresses that trailed on the floor. Grandma received us in her small living room and always served us her own version of Waldorf salad on toast. She always decoratively garnished it with pieces of mandarin orange.   Linn

Serves 4

For the mayonnaise:

2 egg yolks
3 tsp white wine vinegar
1 tsp mustard
salt to taste
7fl oz (200ml) vegetable oil, such as corn oil, canola oil or sunflower oil)
3–4 tbsp heavy cream
pepper

For the salad:

14oz (400g) celery root
2 tart apples (such as Granny Smith apples)
2 tbsp lemon juice
¼ cup shelled walnuts
½ cup mandarin orange segments from a can
salt to taste
pepper
a pinch of sugar to taste

To make the mayonnaise, remove all the ingredients from the refrigerator in advance so that they are at room temperature. Using a hand-held blender, egg beater, or wire whisk, beat the egg yolks with the vinegar, mustard, and salt until everything is well mixed. Beating constantly, add the oil to the eggs a few drops at a time until all the oil has been used. Then beat in the cream so that the mayonnaise does not become too thick. Season with salt and pepper and place in the refrigerator to chill.

To make the salad, wash and peel the celery root and grate it into small sticks. Wash the apples, quarter them, peel them if you like, and remove the cores. Grate the apples. To prevent the celery root and apple from browning, sprinkle them with the lemon juice and place them in a large bowl. Add the mayonnaise and toss well. Set aside 4–6 walnut halves, chop up the rest coarsely, and mix them into the salad.

Thoroughly drain the mandarin segments in a sieve, saving the juice. Stir 1 tablespoon of mandarin juice into the salad. Set aside 8–12 mandarin segments and add the rest to the salad. Toss everything well. Check for seasoning and add salt, pepper, and 1 pinch of sugar as needed. Place the salad in the refrigerator, uncovered, for about 2–4 hours to marinate. Garnish the salad with the mandarin segments and walnut halves and serve.

TIP You can use pears instead of apples, and pineapple instead of mandarins in this salad.

Mainz Cheese Dip

We often rang in the New Year in nearby Mainz at Uncle Heinz and Aunt Lotti's apartment, which was festively decorated with paper garlands and paper snakes. While the adults drank "Cold Duck" and danced with funny paper hats on top of their heads, we, the children, set about the serious task of making a dent in the buffet. Our main focus was the big glass bowl full of Mainz cheese dip — a white, creamy, and delicious dip prepared in the Rhine-Hessen style. Quick as lightning, we gobbled it all up with our small pretzels, much to the dismay of the adults. Birgit

Serves 4
7½oz (200g) cream cheese
7½oz (200g) mild, ripe Camembert cheese
3 tbsp softened, unsalted, butter
1 onion
salt to taste
a pinch of pepper
2 scallions

Place the cream cheese in a bowl and beat it with a fork until it is smooth and creamy. Cut the Camembert into small pieces and fold it and the butter into the cream cheese and blend everything together well. Finely chop the onion and mix it in with the other ingredients in the bowl. Season to taste with salt and pepper. Wash and trim the scallions, cut them into thin rings, and garnish the dip with them.

TIP Mainz cheese dip is best eaten as a snack with fresh whole-grain bread and radishes or with wine and small salty pretzels. The Camembert should not be too strong, otherwise the dish will lose its fresh taste, so choose a mild Camembert. And you have to eat this dip right away, otherwise the raw onions become bitter.

Plaice Finkenwerder Style

Plaice was never served at our house, but I do know this dish from outings our family made to view the apple blossoms in the Alte Land. This is why I always think of it as a spring dish. Of course, plaice can be eaten year-round. Its flesh is firmer in winter; in May, June, and July it is especially tender.   Linn

Serves 4

*4 cleaned plaice
(about 11oz/300g each)
juice of ½ lemon
salt to taste
a pinch of pepper
4½oz (125g) bacon
6 tbsp flour
¼ cup clarified unsalted butter
3 tbsp chopped parsley
4 slices of lemon*

Wash the plaice in cold water and pat them dry. Sprinkle the outside of the fish and the fish cavities with lemon juice. Season the fish inside and out with salt and pepper. Using a sharp knife, cut three diagonal slashes into the dark-skinned sides of the fish. Finely dice the bacon. Put the flour on a large plate, dredge the plaice in the flour on both sides, and shake off the excess flour.

In a large nonstick frying pan, melt the clarified butter. Put the plaice in the frying pan, dark sides down, and fry them over moderate heat for 4 minutes. Turn over the fish and fry them for 3 minutes more until they are done. While they are frying, sauté the diced bacon in a second frying pan over low heat until it has rendered all its fat. Raise the heat and cook the bacon, stirring frequently, until it is golden-brown in color. Arrange the plaice on the plates, white skin side up. Distribute the bacon over the plaice and garnish each with a sprinkling of parsley and a slice of lemon.

TIP For an even more maritime version, use cooked North Atlantic shrimp instead of diced bacon. Warm the shrimp in butter for 2–3 minutes and spoon them over the plaice. Boiled potatoes with butter and, in season, an asparagus salad served with a dressing made of oil, vinegar, and fresh herbs go very well with the plaice.

If plaice are not readily available in your area, substitute 4 small brook trout, adjusting the frying times. You don't have to slash the skin if you are using trout.

Onion Tart

The outdoor pools have closed, the summer tan has faded, and the barbeque has been relegated to the basement. It is fall, time for evening get-togethers with friends in the kitchen. In Germany, it is also time to drink the young, unfermented, wine known as "Federweißer," which goes so well with onion tart. But drinks such as apple cider, both cloudy and clear, Beaujolais Nouveau, or a crisp Riesling wine do very nicely as well. Fall isn't so bad after all!

For 1 baking tray

For the dough:

1lb 2oz (500g) flour
1½oz (42g) yeast cake or
2 tsp active dry yeast
1 pinch of sugar
1 cup lukewarm milk
3 tbsp unsalted butter
1 pinch of salt

For the topping:

6 large onions
9oz (250g) bacon
2 tbsp unsalted butter
7½oz (200g) sour cream
7½fl oz (200g) heavy cream
3 large eggs
1 tbsp cornstarch
1 tsp caraway seeds
½tsp salt

Sift the flour into a large mixing bowl and make a deep well in the center. Crumble the yeast in the well, then add the sugar and 4 tablespoons of the milk. Stirring in the well, carefully incorporate some flour into the liquid. Cover the bowl and leave it in a warm place for 20 minutes until the yeast bubbles up. Melt the butter. Add the remaining milk, salt, and butter to the mixture. Using your hands, knead the flour mixture until it no longer sticks to your fingers, which will take about 3 minutes. Shape the dough into a ball, place it in a bowl, cover, and let it rise in a warm place for 40 minutes until it has almost doubled in volume.

To make the topping, peel the onions and cut them into thin rings. Slice the bacon into very thin strips. Melt the butter in a large frying pan, add the bacon and onions, and sauté them over moderate heat. Remove them from the heat and let cool. Butter a 16×12×1in (40×30×2.5cm) baking tray. Preheat the oven to 375°F (190°C) or 350°F (180°C) on the convection setting. Knead the dough again briefly, place it on a lightly floured work surface and roll it out. Stretch the dough as needed to fit a baking tray, pinching the sides to make a slightly raised edge.

In a bowl, stir together the sour cream, heavy cream, eggs, cornstarch, caraway seeds and salt. Add the cooled onion-and-bacon mixture, stir, and distribute the topping evenly over the dough. Place the baking tray on the middle rack of the preheated oven and bake the tart for 40 minutes. Remove the onion tart from the oven, let it cool down a bit, cut it into pieces, and serve it lukewarm.

Potato Pancakes

After school on Fridays, along with two girlfriends, I would often head over to Grandmother Zick's to eat potato pancakes. On the one hand, Grandmother Zick was feared. Whenever we children would play too loudly and run riot in the courtyard below she would fling open her apartment window high up under the eaves and curse and threaten us. On the other hand, she made the best potato pancakes far and wide. Maybe she just wanted some peace and quiet once a week. We always filled our tummies so full with the delicious, greasy, pancakes that we couldn't even begin to think of running riot, at least not on potato pancake afternoons. Birgit

To make 20 pancakes
1⅓lb (1½kg) white potatoes, such as russet potatoes
1 tsp salt
8–12 tbsp vegetable oil such as canola or sunflower oil

Wash and peel the potatoes and grate them into a bowl using a medium-sized grater. Liberally season the mixture with salt. Use the potato mixture right away, otherwise it turns brown and looks unappetizing!

Heat 6 tablespoons of the oil in a large, heavy, frying pan. For each potato pancake, place 1 heaping tablespoon of the potato mixture in the frying pan and flatten it immediately with the back of a spoon. Fry the pancakes over moderate heat on each side for about 3 minutes until they are cooked on the inside and crispy on the outside. Remove them from the frying pan and place them on paper towels to drain. Repeat this step until all the potato mixture has been used up. Add new oil to the frying pan as needed.

TIP Potato pancakes are also known as potato rösti and latkes. No matter what they are called, they taste best when they are served immediately after they have been fried. When they are kept warm, they lose quite a bit of their crispness. Serve applesauce with the potato pancakes. It has to be cold.

Calf's Liver
with Sautéed Apples

This is one of my husband's favorite meals—but only when it is prepared exactly the way his grandmother used to make it: "The liver was crispy on the outside and tender on the inside—and the onions were dripping with fat that flowed like streams of lava down the mountain of potatoes. That was the absolute best!" Today, some raise their eyebrows at the amount of oil and butter used—but it tastes simply fantastic. And you don't have to eat it every day. Birgit

Serves 4

For the mashed potatoes:

1¾lb (800g) white potatoes, such as russet potatoes
salt
½ cup milk
1 tbsp unsalted butter
1 large pinch of grated nutmeg

For the calf's liver:

2 large onions
salt to taste
1 tsp sugar
5 tbsp sunflower oil
2 tbsp unsalted butter
4 slices calf's liver (about 7½oz (200g) each)
2 tbsp flour
2 large apples
a pinch of pepper

To make the mashed potatoes, peel the potatoes and cut them in half. Place them in a pot with salt and water to cover and bring to a boil. Cook them for about 20 minutes or until they are done. Mash them with a potato masher, then gradually stir in the milk, salt, butter, and nutmeg. Cover and keep warm.

To prepare the calf's liver, preheat the oven to 140°F (60°C). Finely chop the onions. Heat 3 tablespoons of the oil and the 2 tablespoons of butter in a large, heavy, frying pan. Add the onions, salt, and sugar, and sauté the onions slowly until they are soft and nicely browned. Remove them from the frying pan and keep warm. Dredge both sides of the calf's liver in the flour. Heat the remaining 2 tablespoons of oil in the frying pan, add the liver and fry it over high heat for about 1 minute on each side. Remove the frying pan from the heat. Place the liver on a pre-warmed platter and keep warm in the oven.

Peel the apples and core them with an apple corer. Cut them into slices about ⅓in (1cm) thick. Return the frying pan to the heat and sauté the apple slices over moderate heat in the oil and butter used to fry the calf's liver. Remove the liver from the oven, season it with salt and pepper, and place the sautéed apple slices on top. Serve with the mashed potatoes and onions.

TIP You can also make this dish with beef liver, which is much cheaper but doesn't taste quite as outstanding.

Königsberg Meatballs

When I first attempted to make Königsberg meatballs, it seemed so simple. After all, I was using a really good recipe given to me by my husband's grandmother. But there was something missing. The dish tasted boring. I reached for the telephone. "Grandma, what's missing?" There was a moment of silence on the line then she said "Child, you've forgotten the caper water from the jar!" Yes indeed. It is precisely this ingredient that gives the dish the tart, salty, taste that distinguishes Königsberg meatballs from just any meatballs cooked in a white sauce.   Birgit

Serves 4

2 day-old bread rolls

1 large onion

1¾lb (750g) mixed ground meat (such as veal, beef, and pork)

salt to taste

a pinch of pepper

a pinch of grated nutmeg

3 large eggs

2 tbsp unsalted butter

2 heaping tbsp flour

1 cup milk

3½oz (100g) capers from a jar, with their liquid

1 egg yolk

¼ cup heavy cream

½ tsp sugar

1 tsp freshly squeezed lemon juice

Put the bread rolls in water to soften them. Dice the onion finely. Squeeze out the bread to remove excess water. Place the ground meat in a bowl and add the bread rolls, diced onion, salt, pepper, nutmeg, and eggs and knead everything together very well. Moisten your hands and shape the mixture into 20 meatballs.

In a large pot, bring 8½ cups of well-salted water to a boil. Add the meatballs to the water. Turn down the heat so the water barely simmers, and gently poach the meatballs for 10 minutes, making sure the water does not boil. Remove the meatballs. Measure out 2 cups of the cooking liquid and set aside.

Melt the butter in a pot, stir in the flour and cook for a minute or two. Gradually add the milk and poaching liquid, stirring constantly with a wire whisk to prevent lumps from forming. Turn off the heat and let the sauce rest on the burner you have just used, uncovered, for 10 minutes. Stir now and then. Add the capers along with their liquid. Beat together the egg yolk and cream and stir into the sauce. Season with the salt, pepper, sugar, and lemon juice. Put the meatballs in the sauce and gently warm the sauce and meatballs, making sure the sauce does not boil.

TIP An excellent side dish to serve with "Königsberg Meatballs" is a salad of cooked red beets dressed with a pinch of salt, oil, and freshly grated horseradish.

Savoy Cabbage Rolls

This is a sophisticated version of the common cabbage roll. The recipe stems from the Baden area, whose inhabitants are known for their refined taste. Tender Savoy cabbage instead of earthy green cabbage. Creamy tomato sauce instead of bacon sauce. Inside, the rolls are all dressed up with lean ground beef and fresh herbs. It must be Sunday!

Serves 4

8 large Savoy cabbage leaves
2½ tsp salt
1 onion
1lb 2oz (500g) ground beef
1 large egg
2 tbsp bread crumbs
pepper
1 pinch of freshly grated nutmeg
1 tsp fresh thyme leaves
1 tbsp finely chopped flat-leaf parsley
2 tbsp vegetable oil
1 large can peeled, whole, tomatoes (850g)
1 tsp sugar
5 tbsp heavy cream
1 pinch of saffron threads

Wash the cabbage leaves, pat them dry, and trim the center rib of each leaf so it opens flat. Add 1 teaspoon salt to a large pot of water and bring it to a boil. Blanch the cabbage leaves for 2 minutes. Using a slotted spoon, remove the leaves and immediately refresh them in cold water so that they retain their beautiful green color. Drain the leaves. Finely chop the onion.

Mix the ground meat in a bowl with the onion, egg, bread crumbs, 1 teaspoon of salt, and the spices and herbs. Spread out the cabbage leaves on a work surface. Spoon about 2 tablespoons of the ground meat mixture onto each leaf. Starting from the center rib, roll up the leaves, tucking the edges under. Tie the leaves into rolls with kitchen twine. Preheat the oven to 375°F (190°C) or 350°F (180°C) on the convection setting.

Heat the oil in a large frying pan and cook the cabbage rolls on both sides over high heat for about 1 minute. Remove them from the pan and set it aside. Pour the tomatoes into the frying pan, and break them up into small pieces while bringing them to a boil. Add the sugar, the remaining ½ teaspoon of salt, cream, and saffron. Stirring constantly, cook the tomato sauce for about 5 minutes. Pour the sauce into a shallow baking dish. Arrange the 8 cabbage rolls in the dish, pressing them down firmly into the sauce. Place the baking dish on the middle rack of the oven and bake for about 30 minutes.

TIP A smaller, more elegant, version of this dish can be made using spinach leaves. The advantage—the spinach doesn't have to be blanched. The disadvantage—the small, tender, leaves are harder to fill. Make four spinach rolls per person.

Swabian Stuffed Pasta

This is a classic Swabian dish known as "Maultaschen." There's only one true recipe for Swabian meat-filled pasta pouches— and each family has a different one. This particular version was highly recommended to me by the Swabian side of my family. It is best to buy the pasta instead of making it yourself, otherwise the dish is extremely time-consuming to make. Fresh or frozen pasta is available in most supermarkets.   Linn

Serves 4–6

1–2 leeks
7½oz (200g) dry cured salami
1 bunch of flat-leaf parsley
1lb 2oz (500g) uncooked sausage meat
1lb 2oz (500g) mixed ground meat (such as veal and beef)
2 large eggs
salt to taste
a pinch of black pepper
2.2lb (1kg) fresh or frozen large pasta sheets, such as extra-large lasagna sheets

To make the filling, wash and trim the leek and slice it finely. Finely dice the salami. Wash the parsley and chop it finely. Put the uncooked sausage meat in a large bowl. Add the leek, parsley, smoked salami, and eggs and knead the mixture thoroughly. Cook a bit of the mixture in a small frying pan to taste for seasoning. Season to taste with salt and pepper.

Separate the sheets of pasta and lay them out on parchment paper. If needed, cut the sheets so the sheets are square and about 20×28in (50×70cm) in size, or as large as possible. Using a spatula, evenly spread a generous ⅓in (1cm) of filling on each sheet. Next, just as though you were folding a piece of paper, starting at the narrowest edge of the pasta sheet, fold it over carefully to create a strip 2¾in (7cm) wide. Fold this strip over about two more times until all the pasta dough and its filling is folded together flat. This flat method of folding pasta sheets is characteristic of traditional *maultaschen*—Swabian stuffed pasta is not ravioli.

Using a cup, press down very firmly on the filled dough approximately every 4in (10cm). Then, using a knife, cut squares about 3 x 4in (8 x 10cm) in size around the rings you have made. Firmly pinch the cut edges together with your fingers. Repeat until you have used up all the pasta sheets and filling. Bring a large pot of salted water to a rolling boil. Gently place the meat-filled pouches in the water and cook them for 10–15 minutes. When they are done, remove them with a slotted spoon and keep them warm.

TIP Serve Swabian stuffed pasta in beef broth (*see* page 25). You can also serve them as a main course, warmed in melted butter and topped with pan-fried onions along with potato salad (*see* page 89) and a green salad.

Smoked Pork Loin with Sauerkraut

I never imagined I would miss them, those cured pork loin chops particular to Frankfurt, where they are called "Frankfurter Rippchen." They are commonly served in the many Frankfurt restaurants specializing in apple cider. But unless your butcher is originally from Frankfurt, you will have to make do with pork loin chops that are both smoked and cured, unlike the ones from Frankfurt, which are only cured. But both kinds taste delicious, especially with sauerkraut! Birgit

Serves 4

For the sauerkraut:

1 onion
1 apple
1 tbsp clarified unsalted butter or pork lard
1lb 2oz (500g) fresh sauerkraut
1 bay leaf
2 dried juniper berries
1 tsp sugar
1 pinch of salt
½ cup apple cider

For the smoked pork loin chops:

1 small onion
1 bay leaf
1 clove
4 smoked pork loin chops about ½lb (250g) each

To prepare the sauerkraut, peel the onion and dice it finely. Peel and slice the apple. Melt the clarified butter or pork lard in a wide pot. Add the diced onion and sauté it until it is translucent. Add the sauerkraut and continue cooking, separating the sauerkraut a bit using two forks. Add the bay leaf, juniper berries, sugar, salt, and apple and continue to cook everything for about 5 minutes more. Pour in the apple cider, cover the pot, and let everything simmer for about 40 minutes. Stir now and then.

In the meantime, fill a large pot with about 6⅓ cups water and bring it to a boil. Peel the onion and cut a slit into it. Insert the bay leaf into the slit and stick the clove into the onion. Put the onion into the boiling water and cook it for 3 minutes. Next, add the loin chops and cook them for 3 minutes. Reduce the heat and simmer the loin chops for 15 minutes. Turn off the heat and let the loin chops sit for 15 minutes in the water. Remove the loin chops and serve them with the sauerkraut.

TIP Mashed potatoes go very well with this dish as does a piece of thick, crusty bread. And of course, so does a glass of apple cider! If fresh sauerkraut is not readily available in your area, use a can or jar of sauerkraut instead. Drain and rinse the sauerkraut before adding it to the pot.

Sunday Dinners

Vintner Pie

When the exhausting wine harvest was finished, a party was given for all the helpers. The buffet had to include a hearty vintner's pie. There are many regional variations, but this version is always a great hit.   Birgit

Serves 8

For the pie crust:

1lb 2oz (500g) flour
9oz (250g) cold, unsalted, butter, cut into small pieces
1 tsp salt
3 egg yolks
6 tbsp cold water

For the filling:

1lb (500g) uncooked sausages
2 onions
2 garlic cloves
4 pieces white bread
½ cup dry white wine (Riesling or Sylvaner)
1 tbsp fresh marjoram
1 large pinch ground cloves
pepper
salt to taste
10½oz (300g) button mushrooms
1 tbsp unsalted butter
½ bunch flat-leaf parsley

To make the pastry, using your hands, combine the flour, butter, salt, 2 egg yolks and cold water and quickly knead the mixture to make a dough. Gather the dough into a smooth ball, wrap in plastic wrap, and chill for at least 2 hours.

To make the filling, remove the sausage meat from the casings and place it in a bowl. Peel the onions and garlic and chop them finely. Remove the bread crust and crumble the bread. Add the onion, garlic, bread, wine, marjoram, cloves, pepper, and salt to the sausage meat and mix everything together thoroughly. Put the bowl in the refrigerator, uncovered, for 2 hours.

Clean and trim the mushrooms. Melt the butter in a heavy frying pan, add the mushrooms and cook over high heat. Finely chop the parsley, add it to the mushrooms, and season with salt. Continue cooking until the all the liquid has evaporated. Set on one side to cool. Butter a 10-in (26-cm) pie plate. Preheat the oven to 425°F (220°C) or 400°F (200°C) on the convection setting. Set aside a small piece of dough. Roll out two-thirds of the dough and line the pie plate with it, making sure the dough reaches up to the top of the pie plate. Mix the sausage meat and mushrooms together and spread them on the pastry base. Roll out the remaining pastry and drape it over the filling. Firmly pinch together the edges. Cut a hole about ¾in (2cm) in diameter in the pie's center.

Cut leaves from the leftover dough and use to decorate the top of the pie. With the tines of a fork, pierce the top layer of pastry several times. Brush the remaining egg yolk on the top. Bake the pie on the lowest rack of the oven for 30 minutes then move it to the middle rack and bake it for 30 minutes, until it is golden-brown. Let it cool for 30 minutes before serving.

Recipe photo on page 78

Silesian Stew

This unusual dish is our friend Angelika Libera's favorite: "Schlesisches Himmelreich" has an unforgettable aroma—it is salty, sweet, and sour, all at the same time. Even my grandmother and mother, who have lived in Hamburg since the 1960s, cooked this dish to cure their homesickness." Of course, the recipe stems from Theresa, Angelika's mother. Birgit

Serves 4

For the stew:

1⅓lb (600g) smoked pork neck (or lean, smoked, pork belly)
9oz (250g) dried fruit
2 tbsp unsalted butter
2 tbsp flour
1 tbsp sugar
salt to taste
juice of ½ a lemon

For the dumplings:

1lb 2oz (500g) flour
1 tbsp sugar
2 tsp instant yeast
1 cup milk
2 tbsp unsalted butter
salt to taste
1 large egg

To make the stew, put the pork in a pot along with about 6⅓ cups water, bring the water to a boil, and cook the meat over moderate heat for 30 minutes. Add the dried fruit and continue boiling everything for 1 hour more. Remove the meat and dried fruit and keep them warm. Measure out 4¼ cups of the cooking liquid and keep warm.

Melt the butter in a small pot. Stir in the flour and let it cook until light brown in color. Using a soup ladle, and stirring constantly with a wire whisk, gradually beat in the cooking liquid until the sauce is creamy and light-colored. Reduce the heat to its lowest point, cook for 15 minutes, then season to taste with the sugar, salt, and lemon juice.

To make the steamed dumplings, mix together the flour, sugar, and yeast in a bowl. Using a wooden cooking spoon, stir in the milk, butter, salt, and egg until the dough no longer sticks to the sides of the bowl. Moisten a dish towel or a dinner napkin with hot water and wring it out. Spoon the dough into the middle of the dish towel and then roll up the cloth to make a long dumpling. Bind each end of the cloth with kitchen twine to the handle of a long-handled kitchen spoon. Fill a pot with 6⅓ cups of water, add 1 teaspoon of salt, and bring the water to a boil. Hang the cooking spoon across the pot so that the dumpling roll is suspended above the water. Cover the pot and let the dough steam for 45 minutes. Remove the dumplings from the pot. Unroll the dish towel, and, using a sewing thread, cut the dumplings into thick slices. Slice the meat and add it and the dried fruit to the sauce to warm. Serve the sauce with the dumpling slices.

Recipe photo on page 79

81

Kale and Sausage Stew

"Whoever eats kale on New Year's Eve will never lack for money," goes an old saying. Indeed, I've tested the truth of this adage and have to say it's utter nonsense! I even lost a $50 bill on January 1 itself. And one should eat kale much more often than only once at the end of the year because it tastes delicious—especially when combined with smoky, salty, sausage and sweet, caramelized, small potatoes. Birgit

Serves 4

1¾lb (800g) small potatoes
(such as fingerlings or new
potatoes)
salt to taste
3¼lb (1½kg) kale
2 onions
3 tbsp pork lard
or clarified unsalted butter
pepper
1 heaping tbsp sugar
8 sausages, such as mild
chorizo
2 tbsp unsalted butter
mustard to taste

Cook the potatoes in salted water and peel them. Set them aside. Strip the kale leaves from the ribs. Thoroughly wash the kale, changing the water several times until it is clean—kale can be quite sandy. Let it drain in a sieve. Peel the onions and chop them finely. Melt the pork lard or clarified butter in a large pot and sauté the onions until they are translucent. Coarsely chop the kale and add it to the onions. Stirring constantly, briefly cook the kale and onions and season liberally with salt, pepper, and 1 pinch of sugar. Pour in 1 cup of water and stir. Place the sausages on top of the kale. Cover and let simmer on a low heat for 2 hours.

Shortly before the kale is cooked, melt the butter in a large, heavy, frying pan. Add the peeled potatoes and cook them over moderate heat until they are golden-brown. Evenly sprinkle the remaining sugar over the potatoes and, turning them frequently, caramelize them until they are golden-brown. Season with salt. Remove the sausages from the kale and arrange them on a pre-warmed platter with the potatoes. Return the kale to a boil, stirring constantly, boil briefly, and put the kale into a bowl. Serve any kind of mustard you like as a condiment for the sausages.

TIP Instead of or in addition to the sausages (but then only buy two sausages), kale also tastes very good served with smoked pork loin (kasseler). While you are sautéing the onions, brown 4 pieces of smoked pork loin in the lard but take them out of the pan before the onions become translucent. Then place the smoked pork loin and the sausages on top of the kale.

Roulades with Red Cabbage

Unlike their thinner, classic, cousins these roulades are noticeably plump. This is because they are filled with hard-boiled eggs, and not, like classic roulades, with pieces of dill pickle. As a child, I was fascinated when a roulade was cut lengthwise in two and the egg halves appeared. And, because they not only look appealing but also taste fabulous, these roulades are still my favorite — a delicious surprise package. Birgit

Serves 4

For the roulades:

4 large eggs
4 pieces of boneless bottom round beef, 9oz (250g) each pounded to ¼in (6mm)
4 tsp mustard
freshly-ground black pepper
4 slices of bacon
2 large onions
¼ cup vegetable oil
1 bay leaf
1 tsp cayenne pepper
1 tbsp sweet Hungarian paprika
1 tbsp tomato paste
1 tsp sugar
1 tsp salt
1 cup dry red wine
1½ tsp cornstarch

For the red cabbage:

1 red cabbage (about 2.2lb/1kg)
2 tbsp unsalted butter or clarified butter
1 bay leaf
1 cloves
salt to taste
2 tart apples
1–2 tbsp red currant jelly (from a jar)
1–2 tbsp vinegar

Boil the eggs for 8–10 minutes until they are hard cooked. Peel and put them aside. Lay out the pieces of beef side by side and spread each piece with 1 teaspoon of mustard, season with pepper, and cover with 1 slice of bacon. Place a hard-boiled egg in the middle of each piece of beef and roll up the roulade around the filling. Secure the rolls with kitchen twine.

Peel and mince the onions. Heat the vegetable oil in a casserole and sear the beef roulades on all sides—they should be brown but not too dark. Remove the roulades. Add the diced onions, bay leaf, Hungarian paprika, and cayenne pepper to the casserole and cook, stirring constantly. Add the tomato paste, sugar, and salt. Cook for about 1 minute and add the red wine. Return the roulades to the casserole, add 2 cups of hot water, and bring to a simmer. Cover and braise the roulades in the oven at 300°F (150°C) for about 2 hours.

Remove the roulades from the casserole and put them in the oven to keep warm. Pour the cooking liquid into a saucepan through a fine sieve, pressing down on the sieve with the back of a spoon so that all the juices are released. Reheat. If desired, mix the cornstarch with a bit of water until smooth and use it to bind the sauce. Bring the sauce to a simmer and season to taste with salt and pepper. Turn off the heat and return the roulades to the sauce to rest for about 5–10 minutes before serving.

To make the red cabbage, quarter the head of cabbage, remove its core, and shred it finely. Heat the butter in a pot, add the shredded cabbage, and sauté it for about 5 minutes, stirring constantly. Add the bay leaf, clove, salt, and 1¼ cups of water. Cover the pot. Peel and core the apples and cut them into wedges. Place the apple wedges on top of the cabbage and simmer over a low heat for 60 minutes, stirring occasionally. Season the cabbage with enough sugar, salt, red currant jelly, and vinegar to give it an intense sweet-sour flavor. Serve the roulades with red cabbage and potato dumplings (*see* page 94).

Rolled Pasta with Parsley Sauce

My friend Katharina's grandparent's had a huge bed of parsley in their garden. When it was time for the parsley harvest, the whole family had to roll up their sleeves and pick away. But, after it was picked, the parsley still had to be washed (in ice-cold water), the leaves removed from the stems, finely chopped, and packed in portions for freezing. The next day, as a reward for the hours of processing parsley, there was a meal of rolled pasta with parsley sauce!   Linn

Serves 4

2oz (60g) celery root
2oz (60g) carrots
3oz (90g) leek
4 sprigs of parsley
2 chicken legs (about
1lb 2oz/500g)
salt to taste
2¼ cups flour
½tsp baking powder
2 large eggs
5½oz (150g) unsalted butter
5½oz (150g) bread crumbs
2–3 bunches of parsley

To make the parsley sauce, first make the chicken broth. Wash and peel the celery root and carrots and cut them into large pieces. Wash and trim the leek and cut it into slices. Wash the sprigs of parsley, shake them, and pat them dry. Wash the chicken legs and pat them dry. Place the chicken legs and the celery root, carrots, and leeks in a pot and cover with water. Add salt and bring to a boil. Reduce the heat. Cover the pot and gently simmer over moderate heat for about 1 hour. Pour the broth through a sieve and set it aside.

To make the pasta, mix 1lb 2oz (500g) of the flour and the baking powder together and sift them over a bowl. Using a hand mixer, beat the eggs in a large mixing bowl with 1 cup of water and 1 pinch of salt until foamy. Using the dough hook of your mixer, gradually add the flour and knead the dough until it is smooth and elastic. If the dough is still sticky, add a bit of flour. Cover the bowl and chill the dough for 30 minutes.

Slowly melt 3½oz (100g) of the butter in a frying pan. When it is light brown, add the bread crumbs. Stirring constantly, sauté the bread crumbs until they are golden brown, remove them from the heat, and let them cool down a bit. Sprinkle flour on a working surface and roll out the dough into a square (you can also use a pasta maker for this step). Spread the bread crumbs over the dough, leaving the long sides of the dough free. Roll up the pasta dough from the long side. Firmly squeeze the ends together. Cutting across the roll, slice pieces about 1–1½in (3–4cm) thick. Squeeze the open ends together firmly. Add a liberal amount of salt to a pot of water and bring it to a boil. Gently add the filled pasta rolls and boil them for about 20–30 minutes.

Wash the bunches of parsley and shake them dry. Pluck the leaves from the stems and chop them finely. Melt the remaining butter (1¾oz/50g) in a pot, add 2–3 tablespoons of the flour and, using a wire whisk, stir everything together until smooth. Next, stirring constantly so that no lumps form, gradually add about 2 cups of the hot chicken broth until the sauce has the right consistency. Add the parsley and gently cook the sauce over moderate heat for 2 minutes. Remove the sauce from the heat. Season to taste with salt and pepper. Slice the dumplings and serve them with the sauce.

TIP Broth freezes well so you can freeze any leftover broth for another meal. If you prefer, instead of making your own chicken broth, you can also use ready-made vegetable or chicken broth.

Wiener Schnitzel with Potato and Cucumber Salad

It was decades ago when I was first introduced to real Wiener schnitzel. While I was visiting Vienna, a friend took me to a small, rustic, restaurant "Zu den 2 Lieserln." There, without much ceremony, we were served two thin, tender, crispy, golden-brown schnitzels so large that they hung over the edges of the plates. They were served with the classic side dish of lukewarm potato-cucumber salad. I was so impressed—and enthusiastic. In Germany, I'm still looking for a simple local restaurant that serves this dish. But it isn't all that hard to make real Wiener schnitzel—if you pay attention to a few small details, that is. Birgit

Serves 4

For the potato-cucumber salad:

1¾lb (800g) yellow potatoes, such as Yukon gold
1 tsp salt
½ English cucumber
1 cup beef broth
3 tbsp white wine vinegar
5 tbsp sunflower oil
1 tsp medium-hot mustard
1 small onion
1 bunch of chives

For the schnitzels:

4 thinly-cut boneless top round veal cutlets ¼lb (120g) each
a bit of vegetable oil
salt to taste
pepper
freshly grated nutmeg
4 tbsp all-purpose flour
3½oz (100g) fresh bread crumbs
2 large eggs
2 tbsp milk
7½ oz (200g) clarified unsalted butter
4 lemon wedges
cranberry sauce to taste

To make the potato and cucumber salad, wash the potatoes, place them in a pot, and cover with cold water. Add salt. Cover the pot, bring the water to a boil, and cook the potatoes for about 15 minutes until they are done. While they are cooking, peel the cucumber and slice it thinly. Heat the beef broth in a small pot. In a large bowl, combine the vinegar, oil, mustard, and a pinch of salt to make a dressing.

Drain the potatoes, let the steam evaporate, and peel them while they are hot. Cut them into thin slices directly into the dressing. Add the hot broth to the potatoes one-third at a time, tossing carefully after each addition. Wait 10 minutes between each addition to let the potatoes absorb the broth. Finely grate the onion. Chop the chives very finely. When the potato salad is lukewarm, add the cucumber slices, grated onion, and chives.

To make the schnitzels, spread a layer of plastic wrap on a work surface and grease it lightly with the vegetable oil. Place the veal cutlets on the plastic wrap and cover them with another layer of wrap. Carefully flatten the cutlets with a meat pounder until they are about 1/8in (3mm) thick. Strip off the wrap and season the schnitzels on both sides with salt, pepper, and a bit of nutmeg. Place the flour and bread crumbs on two separate plates. In a deeper plate, mix together the milk and the egg.

Heat the clarified butter in a large, heavy, frying pan. Dip each side of the schnitzels into the flour, egg mixture, and bread crumbs. Shake off any excess breading. To get the coveted slightly wavy, bread-crumbed crust, do not press down on the schnitzels! Immediately place the schnitzels in the hot butter and fry them until they are golden brown. They should float in the butter as they fry. Shake the frying pan gently back and forth so that the butter flows over the schnitzel. After about 2–3 minutes, carefully turn each schnitzel and fry it on the other side for 2–3 minutes. Remove the schnitzels from the frying pan and put them on paper towels to drain. Serve with lemon wedges, potato and cucumber salad and, if desired, with a bit of cranberry sauce.

Black Forest Venison

It is said of people from Baden-Württemberg that they are all gourmets. Therefore, it is no surprise that one of the finest venison recipes comes from my friend Sibylle's grandmother who grew up in the Black Forest, which is in Baden-Württemberg. Her roast of venison is marinated in red wine; a fir twig provides a special taste. Birgit

Serves 4

4in (10cm) fir twig
1 onion
1 cup dry red wine
1 bay leaf
4 dried juniper berries
10 black peppercorns
2.2lb (1kg) deboned leg
of venison
½ tsp salt
2 tbsp clarified unsalted
butter
1 tbsp red currant jelly
½ cup sour cream or crème
fraîche
1 tsp cornstarch
2 firm pears
(such as Bosc pears)
juice of ½ a lemon
4 tsp wild cranberry sauce

Wash the fir twig in hot water, shake it, and leave to dry a bit. Peel the onion and chop it coarsely. Make a marinade by pouring the red wine into a bowl and adding the onion, fir twig, bay leaf, dried juniper berries, and peppercorns. Place the venison in the marinade—the meat should be almost fully covered—and cover the bowl. Marinate the meat in the refrigerator for 1–2 days. Turn the meat now and then.

Remove the meat from the marinade, pat it dry, and sprinkle it with salt. Heat the clarified butter in a heavy pot such and sear the roast on all sides. Pour the marinade through a sieve and set it aside. Remove the spices (except for the fir twig) and onion from the sieve, add them to the pot, and cook with the venison for 3 minutes. Pour in the marinade and briefly bring it to a boil, stirring well to loosen the brown crust on the bottom. Cover the pot and braise over low heat for 1½ hours.

Preheat the oven to 165°F (75°C) or 140°F (60°C) on the convection setting. Remove the pot from the heat. Place the venison on a rack in the oven to keep warm. Strain the sauce through a sieve and return it to the pot. Stir in the red currant jelly. Season with salt. Mix the sour cream or crème fraîche with the cornstarch until smooth and bind the sauce with this mixture.

Peel the pears, cut them in half, carefully remove the cores with a teaspoon, and sprinkle them with the lemon juice. Fill a nonstick frying pan with ⅓ in (1cm) of water, add the lemon juice, and bring the water to a boil. Add the pear halves, cut side down, cover, and poach over low heat for about 3 minutes. Remove the pears and fill the hollow of each half with 1 teaspoon of the cranberry sauce. Carve the venison into slices and serve it with the sauce and one 1 pear half per plate.

Hungarian Paprika Chicken

My grandmother was born in Hungary and passed on this recipe to my mother. At some point, my mother began to leave out the chile pepper and cayenne pepper. There was a good reason. When my school friends came to dinner they all found it "wayyy" too hot and would hang their beet-red faces under the faucet for several minutes. Today, the hot pepper is back in there. Birgit

Serves 4

1 red bell pepper
1 green bell pepper
1 large white onion
2 cloves of garlic
1 pinch of salt
3 tbsp vegetable oil
1 chicken, cut into 8 pieces (or 4 chicken legs and 2 chicken breasts bone-in)
salt to taste
pepper
1 dried chile pepper
3 tbsp sweet Hungarian paprika
1 tbsp cayenne pepper
30oz (850g) canned, peeled, tomatoes
¾ cup sour cream
1 tsp cornstarch

Wash the bell peppers, remove the stem, seeds, and the white ribs, and cut each into 8–12 pieces. Peel the onion and dice it finely. Peel the garlic, chop it coarsely, sprinkle it with salt and let it rest for a few minutes. Then, using the flat blade of a heavy knife, crush the garlic. Heat the vegetable oil in a heavy casserole or a large, heavy, frying pan. Over high heat, brown the chicken legs on all sides. Add the pieces of pepper, onion, and garlic, and sauté, stirring constantly. Season with salt and pepper.

Crumble the chile pepper. Stir the chile pepper, paprika, and cayenne pepper into the casserole, making sure the chicken pieces are well coated. Coarsely cut up the tomatoes in the can and pour them along with their juices into the casserole. Stir. Reduce the heat, cover, and cook over low heat for about 40 minutes When the chicken is ready, mix together the sour cream and the cornstarch, pour the mixture into the casserole, and, stirring constantly, return the paprika chicken to a boil to thicken the sauce. Keep the chicken warm until you are ready to serve. Thick egg noodles go very well with this dish. If you want to make your own egg noodles, try the spätzle recipe on page 44 (but omit the cheese). Cook the spätzle in boiling, salted, water and serve them with the paprika chicken.

Rhine Sauerbraten with Potato Dumplings

My friend Gabi, who grew up near Cologne, had a special relationship with sauerbraten: after her parents had a fight, they often didn't speak one word to each other for days. For Gabi, a reliable signal that hostilities were over was the aroma of sauerbraten wafting through the house—her mother always made this dish as a kind of peace-offering. Birgit

Serves 4

For the sauerbraten:

1 carrot
1 large onion
2 cups water
1 cup red wine vinegar
4 cloves
10 dried juniper berries
10 allspice berries
1 tsp white peppercorns
1 bay leaf
2.2lb (1kg) boneless beef bottom round
1 tsp salt
1 tsp pepper
3 tbsp vegetable oil
3oz (80g) raisins
1 tsp cornstarch if desired
honey or sugar to taste

For the potato dumplings:

2.2lb (1kg) white potatoes, such as russet potatoes
salt
3½oz (100g) flour
a bit of freshly grated nutmeg
2 large eggs

Wash the carrot, peel the onion, and dice them finely. Place the vinegar, water, and carrots in a pot, and bring to a boil. Add the cloves, dried juniper berries, allspice berries, pepper, and bay leaf and stir. Remove the marinade from the heat and cool it down. Put the venison in a large bowl, pour the marinade over it, cover, and marinate the meat in the refrigerator for 3 days, turning it now and then—sauerbraten is not a dish for impromptu dinner invitations!

Remove the meat from the marinade, pat it dry, and season it with salt. Pour the marinade through a sieve, retaining the marinade and vegetables. In a heavy casserole, heat the vegetable oil and sear the meat on all sides. Add the marinade vegetables and spices. Pour 1 cup of the marinade into the casserole, stirring to loosen the brown bits on the bottom. Boil the sauce briefly and reduce the heat. Cover the casserole and gently simmer the roast over low heat for about 2 hours, turning it now and then. If needed, add a bit of water.

To make the potato dumplings, boil the potatoes in salted water. Let the steam evaporate and peel the potatoes while they are still hot. Immediately put them through a potato ricer into a bowl. Cover and chill. Once they are cool, sprinkle the flour over the potatoes and season them with ½ teaspoon salt and the

nutmeg. Beat the eggs and mix them into the potato dough. Using your hands, knead the dough until it is smooth and elastic. If the dough is too soft, add a bit of flour. Shape 12 dumplings and slide them gently into boiling, salted, water. Return to a boil, reduce the heat, and simmer the dumplings for 20 minutes. Remove them from the pot and keep them warm.

Preheat the oven to 165 °F (75 °C) or 140 °F (60 °C) on the convection setting. Remove the sauerbraten from the casserole and put it in the oven to keep warm. Strain the roasting liquid through a sieve and pour it back into the casserole. Add the raisins and reduce the sauce to about 1 cup. If desired, mix the cornstarch with a bit of water in a cup and use it to bind the sauce. Season to taste with honey or sugar and salt and pepper. Serve the sauerbraten with the potato dumplings and applesauce.

TIP Instead of a bowl, use a leakproof freezer bag to marinate the meat. Since the meat is submerged in the marinade, it doesn't need turning.

95

Boiled Beef with Horseradish Sauce

Beef is boiled to make the soup course of this traditional Sunday meal. Then, for the main course, the beef is sliced and served with Savoy cabbage, horseradish sauce, and pan-fried potatoes.   Birgit

Serves 6

3⅓lb (1½kg) cooked beef from the beef soup recipe on page 25

For the Savoy cabbage:

1 head of Savoy cabbage about 3⅓lb (1½kg)
salt to taste
1 small onion
2 tbsp unsalted butter
1½ tbsp flour
½ cup beef broth (see page 25)
freshly grated nutmeg

For the horseradish sauce:

1¾oz (50g) freshly grated horseradish
5 tbsp milk or heavy cream
3 tbsp unsalted butter
¾oz (20g) flour
¾ cup heavy cream
¾ cup beef broth (see page 25)
salt to taste
a bit of black pepper
freshly grated nutmeg
a pinch of sugar

To prepare the Savoy cabbage, remove the leaves from the head of cabbage. Cut out the thick middle ribs and slice the leaves into strips. Wash and drain the cabbage. In a large pot, bring salted water to a boil. Add the cabbage and cook it for about 15 minutes until it is tender. Drain it in a sieve, catching the cooking liquid in a bowl. Finely chop the cooked cabbage using a knife or the coarsest disk of a meat grinder. Peel and mince the onion. Melt the butter in a pot, add the onions, and sauté them slowly until they are translucent but not brown. Add the flour and cook, stirring constantly with a wire whisk. Pour in the beef broth and 1 soup ladle of the cabbage cooking liquid and mix well until the flour mixture is smooth. Add the cabbage, mix it in thoroughly, and cook it for 5 minutes, stirring often. Season it to taste with salt and nutmeg.

To make the horseradish sauce, peel and chop the horseradish root and purée it in the blender together with the milk or heavy cream. Melt the butter in a pot, add the flour, and stir constantly over low heat—the flour should not become brown. Pour in the cream and beef broth and stir until smooth. Add the puréed horseradish and season the sauce with salt, pepper, nutmeg, and sugar. Cook the sauce for 10 minutes over moderate heat, stirring often. To serve, remove the cooked beef from the broth, cut it into slices, and arrange it on a pre-warmed platter. Sprinkle a bit of salt and 3–4 tablespoons of the beef broth over the meat. Serve the beef with the horseradish sauce, Savoy cabbage, and pan-fried potatoes (*see* page 37).

Walburga Maier from Bavaria

A Passion for Herbs

If you ask Walburga Maier whether she sometimes leaves her idyllic farm in the Chiemgau—to go to Munich for example, or on excursions—she shakes her head and says: "I don't have any time for that!" For even though her son and daughter-in-law have long since taken over the task of running the farm, with its cows, fertile fields, and vacation apartments, the former farmer's wife still has no time to rest. From morning to night she toils in her garden, weeding the herb bed, planting fruit and vegetables, cooking jam, or drying various leaves for her herbal teas. She even makes her own liquors. There are twelve kinds on the shelves of the large old pantry, such as dandelion or rosehip liquor. And of course, she has picked and gathered everything herself. A trained guide, Walburga also leads guided walks once a week to teach the vacation guests, both young and old, about herbs.

From her kitchen window, Walburga Maier has a clear view of her beloved garden. Beyond, the mountains are picturesquely etched against the sky just like on a postcard. Here, in the kitchen, it is especially cozy since the old wood-burning stove has been stoked to make us her delicious roast pork. No, going away on vacation is something she can't even contemplate doing. Who would take care of her garden then? But a few years ago, Walburga received a gift certificate for an Ayurvedic cooking course which she'd like to redeem. The teacher is a chef from India who runs a cooking school on the Fraueninsel, an island in Lake Chiemsee. "But not just now," Walburga says, already off and running. "Perhaps in September. We'll see!"

Bavarian Roast Pork

For decades, Walburga Maier has made this wonderful, juicy, pork roast with crackling for her family, served with bread dumplings and potato salad. And there's also always a green salad to go with it. When we visited her in Lugingerhof near Lake Chiemsee, she also made her special roast of pork for us— live, with all the bells and whistles, to admire and take notes! Birgit

Serves 4–6

3 tbsp vegetable oil
3lb 5oz (1½kg) deboned pork shoulder, with rind
½lb (200g) uncooked pork belly in one piece
salt and pepper to taste
½ tsp caraway seeds
2 onions
1 clove of garlic
1 handful of parsley leaves
4¼ cups beef broth
a few leaves of mugwort
the crust of 1 slice of pumpernickel or rye bread
1 tsp salt
1 tsp cornstarch

Preheat the oven to 400°F (200°C). Heat the vegetable oil in a heavy-bottomed roasting pan. Over high heat, sear the pork and the pork belly on all sides. Take the meat out of the roasting pan and season it with pepper, salt, and caraway seeds. Return the meat to the roasting pan, placing the rind side down. Peel and chop the onions and garlic. Wash and chop the parsley. Place the onions in the roasting pan and sauté them until they are translucent. Add 2 soup ladles of broth, the garlic, parsley, mugwort and bread crust to the meat. Place the roasting pan on the middle rack of the oven and roast the pork for 30 minutes.

Take the roasting pan out of the oven, turn over the piece of pork, and slice the pork rind into diamonds with a very sharp knife. Return the roasting pan to the oven and roast the pork for 1 hour more, uncovered, adding 1 soup-ladle of broth now and then. Dissolve 1 teaspoon of salt in a bit of water and brush it over the pork rind. Return the roast to the oven to cook for 30 minutes more. Take the roasting pan out of the oven and turn off the oven. Remove the pork from the roasting pan and keep it warm. Set the pork belly aside. Over moderate heat, boil the juices in the roasting pan to loosen the drippings, stirring well. Add a bit more beef broth if needed. Next, pour the sauce through a sieve and return it to the roasting pan and bind it with the cornstarch. Return the liquid to a boil for the last time and taste for seasoning. Cut the roast into slices, pour the sauce into a gravy boat, and serve.

TIP Walburga Maier serves salad, a Bavarian potato salad with vinegar-oil dressing, and bread dumplings (see page 49) with the roast pork.

Trout with Almond Butter

How can one fish taste so very different? Freshly-caught trout poached in fish broth, with its blue-toned, shimmering, skin was a dish I was never particularly fond of. On the other hand, this crispy version, pan-fried in almond butter, is my favorite fish dish. Linn

Serves 4

*4 cleaned trout
(about ¾lb/350g each)
juice of ½ a lemon
salt to taste
a bit of black pepper
5 tbsp flour
3 tbsp unsalted butter
3½oz (100g) sliced almonds
4 wedges of lemon*

Wash the trout with cold water and pat it dry. Rub the fish with lemon juice and season it with salt and pepper. Place the flour on a large plate and dip both sides of the trout in the flour. Shake off any excess flour. Melt the butter in a large, heavy, frying pan, reserving about ½ tablespoon to fry the almonds in later.

Fry the trout one after the other over moderate heat for about 5 minutes on each side until they are golden-brown. In a second frying pan, melt the reserved butter. Add the almonds, and cook them until they are light brown. Arrange the trout on the plates, pour the almond butter over them, and garnish the plates with slivered almonds and lemon wedges.

TIP Small boiled parslied potatoes go very well with the trout. If you would like a plainer version, simply leave out the almonds! When you buy the fish, make sure the skin is shiny and the eyes are clear. And, a well-developed tail-fin is a sign that the trout has had enough room in the water to swim.

Roast Duck with Brussel Sprouts and Chestnuts

Chestnuts—the edible kind—grow in the woods of the Taunus mountains around Kronberg and Königstein. In the fall, you easily can gather the ripe fruit from the ground, score them, roast them in the oven until they are soft inside and then nibble on the peeled chestuts with a glass of wine. Or, just like my friend Gudrun's grandmother does, you can serve them as an accompaniment to a superb roast duck.   Birgit

Serves 4–6

For the duck:

1 apple
1 carrot
1 onion
½ bunch thyme
salt
1 oven-ready duck, with gizzards, about 5½lb (2½kg)
1 cup chicken broth
⅓ cup white wine
¼ cup heavy cream
a pinch of black pepper
a pinch of sweet Hungarian paprika

For the Brussel sprouts and chestnuts:

1⅓lb (600g) Brussel sprouts (fresh or frozen)
salt to taste
1lb 2oz (500g) peeled and roasted chestnuts
1 pinch of freshly grated nutmeg
1 pinch of sugar
7 tbsp unsalted butter

Core the apple. Peel the apple, carrot, and onion and cut into chunks. Wash the thyme. Dissolve 1 teaspoon salt in ½ cup warm water. Brush the duck on all sides with the salt water. Season the pieces of apple with salt and mix in a few thyme leaves. Stuff the duck with the apples and loosely place the remaining thyme into the bird's cavity. Insert the wingtips into slots in the skin on the duck's sides. Selecting both top and bottom heat, preheat the oven to 350°F (180°C) or 325°F (170°C) on the convection setting.

Place the onion, carrot, and the duck gizzards (except for the liver) in the oven's dripping pan and put the pan on the lowest level of the oven. Insert the wire oven rack directly above and place the duck on the rack with the breast side up. After about 30 minutes, pour 1 cup of hot water into the dripping pan and immediately close the oven door. Roast the duck for about 3 hours until it is beautifully golden brown and its skin is crispy. If you do not have convection heat, you will have to turn over the duck half-way into the cooking time. Now and then, brush the duck with saltwater—this is what gives the duck its crispy skin. Pour water into the dripping pan as needed.

Fifteen minutes before serving, pour the dripping pan's contents into a sieve set over a saucepan. Remove the gizzards and set aside. Using the back of a spoon, press the roasted vegetables through the sieve into the pan juices and discard the rest. Remove the layer of fat from the sauce with a spoon. Pour the broth and the white wine into a saucepan, bring the sauce to a boil and add the cream. If the sauce is too thin, reduce. Season to taste with the salt, pepper, and paprika.

While the duck is roasting, clean the Brussel sprouts and cook them in a large pot of boiling salted water for 12 minutes. Drain and shock them by plunging them into ice-cold water. Combine the Brussel sprouts and chestnuts in a pot, season with salt, nutmeg, and sugar. Ten minutes before serving, brown the butter in a small frying pan, pour it over the Brussel sprouts and chestnuts and stir carefully. Reheat the vegetables on low, stirring now and then. Season with salt and nutmeg. Place the stuffing on a pre-warmed platter with the roasted duck and surround the duck with some of the vegetables. Serve the sauce and the remaining vegetables separately.

TIP White country style bread or potato dumplings (*see* page 94) go well with this dish. Duck fat is tasty on bread and gives an extra flavor boost to vegetables. For a delectable first course, cook the duck liver in a bit of butter or duck fat until it is crispy, sprinkle it with salt and pepper, set it on a piece of toast, and enjoy! It's simply delicious!

Sweet Main Courses
& Desserts

Elderflower Soup with Semolina Pudding

My best friend Tiffany grew up in France. In summer, her grandparents would visit from Hamburg. She explains why this is her favorite recipe, telling us: "During the summer holidays, my grandmother prepared this elderflower soup using berries she had picked herself. The whole house smelled of this fruit soup when she was there. It was hot, and school was going to start again soon—but it was still summer vacation. And, somehow, time seemed to stand still." Linn

Serves 4

For the semolina pudding:

2 cups milk
1 pinch of salt
1¾oz (50g) sugar
½ vanilla bean
1in (3cm) cinnamon stick
2½oz (70g) semolina
1 large egg

For the elderflower soup:

1½ tbsp cornstarch
3¼ cups elderflower juice
2 apples
2 tbsp sugar

To make the semolina pudding, bring the milk, salt, sugar, vanilla bean, and cinnamon stick to a boil in a pot. Remove the vanilla bean and cinnamon. Stirring constantly, slowly pour the semolina into the milk and cook it over low heat for 2–3 minutes until the pudding starts to thicken. Remove the pot from the heat and beat the egg into the still-hot mixture. Pour the pudding into a bowl and let it cool for about 1 hour.

To make the elderflower soup, mix the cornstarch with ⅓ cup of the elderflower juice. Peel and core the apples and cut them into slices. Place the rest of the elderflower juice, apple slices, and sugar into a pot and bring to a boil. Stirring constantly, add the cornstarch mixture to the juice and cook for 2–3 minutes more until the soup has thickened and the apples are tender. Ladle the soup into soup bowls. Using two tablespoons, carve out little dumplings from the cold semolina pudding and place 3 or 4 in each bowl of hot soup.

Recipe photo on page 106

TIP If you would like to turn out the semolina pudding, rinse a bowl with cold water before filling it with the pudding mixture. Run a knife along the edge of the pudding to loosen it from the bowl and turn it out onto a plate.

Kaiserschmarrn

No matter how full you are, there's always room for this classic Austrian dish, a kind of topsy-turvy pancakes. This is one of my favorites going back to childhood. Of the many versions, some of which are complicated, this one is simple to make and a keeper.   Birgit

Serves 4

5 *extra-large eggs*
1 *cup heavy cream*
2 *tbsp sugar*
1¾oz (50g) *raisins*
7oz (200g) *flour*
1 *pinch of salt*
4 *tbsp unsalted butter*
confectioner's sugar

Separate the eggs. Whip the cream, egg yolks, sugar, raisins, flour, and salt together in a bowl to make a batter. In a second bowl, whip the egg whites with a pinch of salt until they form stiff peaks. Fold the egg whites into the batter. In a large frying pan, melt 2 tablespoons of the butter over medium heat. Pour in half of the batter. As soon as the batter starts to set, chop it up coarsely and turn it in the pan. Then, using two wooden or nonstick spatulas, tear apart the pancake into bite-sized pieces and continue cooking until it is golden-brown. Repeat with the rest of the batter, dust with the confectioner's sugar, and serve.

Recipe photo on page 107

TIP The pancakes are always torn apart, never cut! If you would like a crispier version, omit the sugar from the batter. Then, after you have turned over the pancake and torn it apart, sprinkle the pieces with 1–2 tablespoons of sugar and cook until it is slightly caramelized. Serve it with applesauce.

Crêpes filled with Quark

In our house, my father was always responsible for making these filled crêpes—after all, he had lived in Austria for a few years and this dish is even more popular in Austria than it is in Germany. He made them for us so often that he could almost make them in his sleep!   Birgit

Serves 4

9oz (250g) quark (alternatively, use thick and creamy, plain, non-fat yogurt)
¾ cup milk
3½oz (100g) flour
1 pinch of salt
3 tbsp sugar
4 large eggs
4 tbsp confectioner's sugar
1 tsp pure vanilla extract
juice of ½ lemon
½ tsp zest of an organic lemon
3–4 tbsp unsalted butter
a few raspberries
a bit of confectioner's sugar

Drain the quark or yogurt in a fine sieve set over a bowl. To make the batter, pour the milk into a bowl. Using a wire whisk, stir in the flour and salt. Let the batter rest for 30 minutes. Then, beat in the sugar and eggs and set the batter aside. To make the filling, put the drained quark or the yogurt in a bowl. Beat in the confectioner's sugar, vanilla extract, lemon juice, and lemon zest until the mixture is free of lumps. Set the filling aside.

Melt 1 tablespoon of butter in a frying pan. Pour in 1 small soup ladle of batter into the pan and tilt the pan to evenly spread the batter. Cook the crêpe over moderate heat, until it is golden-brown underneath. Gently turn it over and brown the other side. Place the crêpe on a plate. Melt a bit more butter in the frying pan and continue making the pancakes until all the batter is used up (the batter should yield about 6–8 crêpes). Spread each crêpe evenly with the filling, roll it up, and cut it on an angle into thick slices. Distribute it on plates, garnish with a few raspberries, and dust with confectioner's sugar.

TIP These crêpes also taste delicious baked in the oven. Tightly place the filled and rolled up pancakes in a buttered baking dish. Preheat the oven to 425°F (220°C). Mix 1 cup of crème fraîche, 2 teaspoons of confectioner's sugar, and 1 egg yolk in a small bowl and pour the mixture over the crêpes. Place the baking dish on the middle rack of the oven. Bake for about 10 minutes.

Sweet Main Courses & Desserts

Apple, Rice, and Meringue Pudding

This delicious dessert was often served by my godmother, Aunt Emilie, whose dining room table was usually full of hungry diners. Once, when this pudding, which I really loved, was being served there were at least ten people at the table. As the bowl was passed around each guest took a heaping portion. Unfortunately, little Birgit was sitting almost at the end of the table. As the bowl grew emptier and emptier my eyes grew wider and wider. Suddenly, I jumped up and shouted "Stop!" Everyone laughed—and I was allowed, finally, to fill my plate. Birgit

Serves 4–6
9oz (250g) short-grain rice
6 tbsp sugar
1 pinch of salt
1 piece of lemon, peeled and pith removed
4¼ cups milk
2.2lb (1kg) apples, peeled
juice of ½ lemon
2 tbsp unsalted butter
3 egg whites

In a tall pot, bring the rice, 2 tablespoons of sugar, the salt, the piece of lemon, and the milk to a boil over low heat. Stirring constantly, cook the rice for about 15 minutes. Peel and core the apples and chop them into small pieces. Sprinkle the apple pieces with the lemon juice immediately to prevent them from turning brown. Melt the butter in a large pot, add the apples and 2 tablespoons of the sugar, and cook until the apples are tender. Spread a layer of rice pudding in a round casserole dish with a high rim. Evenly distribute the pieces of apple over the rice, then layer the remaining rice over the apples

Preheat the oven to 350 °F (180 °C). Using a rotary mixer, beat the egg whites in a bowl with 2 tablespoons of sugar until they form stiff peaks. Spread the egg whites over the rice. Place the casserole on the middle rack of the oven and bake for about 5–10 minutes until the meringue is lightly browned. Watch out that the meringue doesn't burn—this can happen very quickly!

TIP If you would like to serve this dish for dessert after a special meal, make it in individual portions as shown in the photograph. Use small ovenproof glass dishes. But spread just one layer of rice at the bottom, then top the rice with a layer of apples and top the apples with the meringue.

Rote Grütze (Red-Berry Pudding)

On hot summer days at my grandmother's, a plate of red berry pudding with milk was always served at lunchtime. It was wonderfully refreshing! However, it was hard to get my grandmother to provide us with a detailed recipe since she never weighed the ingredients. But she finally did so as a favor to us. Definitely try the pudding with the vanilla custard on page 116! Linn

Serves 8

2.2lb (1kg) mixed fresh berries, such as 9oz (250g) each red currants, raspberries, strawberries, and blueberries

2 cups red fruit juice (such as cherry juice)

1¾oz (50g) cornstarch

3½oz (100g) sugar

Wash the berries. Pick through them carefully and remove any damaged fruit. Set the berries aside. Measure out about ½ cup of the cherry juice into a small bowl and stir in the cornstarch until the mixture is smooth. In a pot, bring the rest of the juice to a boil and reduce the heat. Stirring constantly, slowly add the cornstarch mixture and the sugar. Continue stirring until the juice begins to thicken.

Add the berries, preferably adding tougher-skinned fruit first, such as the red currants. If you are using raspberries, stir these in last since they fall apart the quickest. Bring the pudding and the berries to a boil and cook everything briefly. Taste the pudding (be careful, it will be very hot). If needed, add a bit of sugar. If the pudding is sweet enough, remove it from the heat immediately. You don't want the berries to fall apart. To serve, pour into a large glass bowl or into individual bowls.

TIP When sweet cherries, such as Bing cherries, are ripe, you must try them in the pudding. Make sure the cherries are unblemished and firm. You will have to pit them. In late summer, the first ripe plums and prunes also make a wonderful addition. Also delicious is a yellow berry pudding made with small yellow plums (such as mirabelle plums), apricots, or peaches. These fruits will have to be peeled.

Chocolate Pudding

When I was a child, the nicest thing about my grandmother's cooking skills was that she always made a dessert at lunchtime. And it was usually a pudding. Jello, vanilla pudding, or even this ultra-chocolatey chocolate pudding were high up on my hit list. It was crucial that the pudding was drowned in vanilla custard. For this reason, here is a recipe that includes the world's best vanilla custard, which also goes really well with baked apples, steamed dumplings, and red berry pudding!   Linn

Serves 2–4

For the pudding:

1½oz (40g) cornstarch
2 cups milk
4 tbsp sugar
1 pinch of ground vanilla (or ½ tsp pure vanilla extract)
1 egg yolk
3½oz (100g) dark chocolate

For the vanilla custard:

2 egg yolks
4¼ cups milk
1½oz (30g) cornstarch
2oz (60g) sugar
1 vanilla bean

To make the chocolate pudding, using a wire whisk, mix the cornstarch together with 6 tablespoons of milk, the sugar, and the vanilla in a bowl until smooth. In a second bowl, beat the egg yolks. Break the chocolate into pieces, place them in a pot with the remaining milk and bring everything to a boil. Stir in the cornstarch mixture and cook for about 3 minutes until the pudding thickens. Remove the pot from the heat and beat in the egg yolk. Pour the pudding immediately into a heatproof bowl rinsed in cold water and let it cool.

To make the vanilla custard, using an electric hand mixer, beat the egg yolks in a bowl until they are thick and creamy. In a small bowl, mix 6 tablespoons of the milk with the cornstarch until smooth. Place the remaining milk and the sugar in a pot. Slit open the vanilla bean. Using the handle of a spoon, scrape out the seeds into the milk. Place the vanilla pod in the milk. Stirring constantly, bring everything to a boil. Remove the vanilla pod and beat in the cornstarch mixture. Boil for 2 minutes, stirring constantly, until the custard has thickened. Remove it from the heat. Beat in the egg mixture, return it to the heat, and let the custard boil up for about 30 seconds. Remove from the heat, pour into a gravy boat, and enjoy either hot or cold.

TIP To make this pudding for children, use 3½oz (100g) of milk chocolate or white chocolate instead of dark chocolate and reduce the amount of sugar by 1–2 tablespoons.

Baked Apples with Marzipan

Outside, the first strong fall winds are gusting through the streets and the rain is pattering on the windowpanes. Inside, it seems even cozier, with our grandmother's old black-and-white photos in the faded photo album and the sweet-sour, baked apples with vanilla custard (see page 116) hot from the oven. It's just like being in a fairy tale.

Serves 4
1½oz (40g) unsalted butter
4 tart apples such as Granny Smith
3½oz (100g) almond paste
1oz (20g) raisins
1 pinch of ground cinnamon
1½oz (30g) sliced or slivered almonds

Preheat the oven to 400°C (200°C). Butter a casserole dish. Melt the butter. Wash the apples and core them using an apple-corer. Knead together the almond paste, raisins, cinnamon, and slivered almonds. Spoon this mixture into the cored apples and garnish to taste with slivered almonds. Set the apples in the casserole dish and brush them with the melted butter. Place the dish on the middle rack of the preheated oven and bake for 25 minutes.

Arme Ritter (French Toast)

White bread famously dries out after only 1–2 days, but you certainly don't have to throw it away. Leftover bread is ideal for making sweet baked desserts such as cherry bread pudding, bread dumplings, and meat patties. And the most delicious way of all to use up leftover white bread is to make French toast, which is known as "Arme Ritter" (poor knight) in Germany!

Makes 5 pieces
3 large eggs
⅔ cup milk
⅓ cup heavy cream
1 pinch of salt
1 tsp pure vanilla extract
5 slices day-old white bread
1 tbsp unsalted butter
a pinch of cinnamon
1 tsp confectioner's sugar

Put the eggs, milk, cream, salt, and vanilla extract in a bowl and beat with a fork or wire whisk. Place the pieces of white bread, which should be about ¾in (2cm) thick, in the milk-and-egg mixture and let the bread absorb the liquid for 10 minutes until saturated. Melt the butter in a frying pan. Over moderate heat, cook the slices of bread on both sides until they are golden-brown. Sprinkle with a bit of cinnamon and confectioner's sugar as desired.

No recipe photo

Doris Gretzinger from Swabia

Swabian Kitchen Classics

Doris Gretzinger from Baden-Württemberg always has time for her grandchildren. Although most of them are grown up now and no longer spend summer vacations with her, they still think their favorite dishes, such as steamed dumplings with vanilla custard, are unbeatable. When the family visits, Doris serves them tried-and-true dishes such as schupf noodles, spätzle with sour beans, and applesauce, and of course everything is made from scratch. At coffee klatsches and on vacation, her hazelnut torte, cinnamon rolls, and other sweet temptations are very much in demand. Even today, her grandchildren don't think birthday parties are complete without their grandmother's fruit tarts. During the Swabian carnival season, Doris always goes to watch the parades of fools—and her sweet carnival cake is part of the carnival celebration. And what would Christmas be without a large jar of grandma's wonderful traditional Swabian Christmas cookies? She is a veritable master baker of these, and can make over a dozen kinds.

Doris is also proud of her rare Upper-Swabian specialities such as fried "cigar noodles" made of potato dough, or green donuts filled with bacon and spring onions. She buys her vegetables and fruit at the market and so always has some seasonal food on the table. And on her balcony, Doris grows salad leaves and herbs in containers placed between pots of impatiens and black-eyed Susan. On Fridays, Doris has little time to spend with visitors since this is her weekly bowling day. She also tours the beautiful countryside full of meadow orchards and Baroque churches with her bowling friends and the railway seniors' club. In her hometown Biberach on the Riß river, there isn't a path she doesn't know. On her daily walks there is always time for a nice chat when she runs into an acquaintance, and she always does!

Steamed Dumplings

One needs good hearing to make steamed dumplings. As Doris Gretzinger says, you can hear it when a good salty crust has formed—the dumplings crackle slightly. The pot must have a close-fitting lid and, no matter what the temptation, must stay closed when the dumplings are cooking, otherwise they will not turn out round and light but small and hard. This is not a recipe for the curious or impatient!

Serves 4
1lb 2oz (500g) flour
1½oz (42g) yeast cake or
2 tsp active dry yeast
1 pinch of sugar
1 cup milk
1 large egg
1½ tsp salt
3 tbsp unsalted butter

Sift the flour into a bowl and make a deep well in the center. Crumble the yeast in the well, then add the sugar and 4 tablespoons of the milk. Stirring in the well, carefully incorporate a bit of flour into the liquid. Cover the bowl and leave it in a warm place for 20 minutes until the yeast bubbles up. Add the remaining milk, the egg, and ½ teaspoon of the salt to the dough. Using your hands, knead the dough until it no longer sticks to your fingers. This takes about 3–4 minutes. Shape the dough into 8 balls, place them on a floured work surface, and let them rise for 40 minutes more.

Bring 2 cups of salted water to a boil in a wide pot and add the butter. When the butter has melted, place the balls of dough in the water. Cover the pot with a tight-fitting lid and simmer over low heat for about 20 minutes. Do not remove the lid! The dumplings are ready when the liquid has evaporated and a crust has formed on the bottom of the dumplings. You can hear it when a crust has formed because the dumplings crackle a bit. Remove the pot from the heat. Using two spoons, take the steamed dumplings out of the pot and serve.

TIP These taste best with vanilla custard (page 116) or homemade fruit compote. The next day, any leftover dumplings are sliced and fried in a frying pan with diced bacon and served, for example, with butter mixed with herbs.

123

Kirschenmichel
(Cherry Bread Pudding)

In summer, when the dark-red cherries hung juicy and ripe on the trees, I knew that cherry bread pudding time had arrived again. For this pudding was only made during the fairly short time the cherries were ripe. To make sure it was served as often as possible, I helped — with a great deal of enthusiasm and not much precision — to pit the cherries, ensuring everyone was guaranteed biting into at least one cherry stone. I always maintained that it was these pits that gave the cherry cobbler its special taste.   Birgit

Serves 4–6

1¾lb (750g) sweet cherries, such as Bing cherries
5 day-old bread rolls
2 cups milk
2 large eggs
3 tbsp softened unsalted butter
6 tbsp sugar
1 tsp zest of 1 organic lemon
1 pinch of baking powder
2 heaping tbsp flour
1 tbsp bread crumbs
a few small pieces of butter

Pit the cherries and set them on one side. Slice the bread rolls into slices ⅓in (1cm) thick and soak them in the cold milk. Separate the eggs. Using a wire whisk, whisk the butter, 5 tablespoons of the sugar and the egg yolk in a bowl until thick and creamy. Mix in the lemon zest, baking powder, flour, and milk-soaked bread. In a second bowl, using an electric hand-mixer, beat the egg whites until they form stiff peaks and fold them into the mixture.

Preheat the oven to 375°F (190°C) or 350°F (180°C) if you are using convection heat. Butter a square casserole dish. Spread a layer of the cherries on the bottom of the dish, then a layer of the bread-and-egg mixture. Continue alternating layers until all the ingredients are used up. Sprinkle the top layer with the bread crumbs and dot it with a few pieces of butter. Place the bread pudding on the middle rack of the preheated oven and bake it for about 45 minutes until it is golden-brown. Remove it from the oven, sprinkle it with the remaining 1 tablespoon of sugar, and serve immediately.

TIP Cherry bread pudding has to be eaten fresh from the oven. When the pudding is cold, it loses much of its fluffiness and only tastes half as good as when it is hot.

Quarkkäulchen
(Quark Potato Cakes)

Are they sweet or salty? Do you call them potato cakes or potato pancakes? Do you add potatoes or only use flour? There are many questions about this dish and there's no one perfect answer. So a quark potato pancake is a real chameleon. It changes its shape and taste as it pleases. Our recipe comes from my friend Therese's Saxon grandmother. Even as a child, Therese could not get enough of these pan-fried cakes. They are sweet, made with potatoes and flour, and definitely unique. Birgit

Serves 4

1lb 2oz (500g) potatoes
salt to taste
1lb 2oz (500g) quark (alternatively, use thick and creamy, plain, non-fat yogurt
3½oz (100g) flour
4 tbsp sugar
1 large egg
a bit of freshly grated nutmeg
1 tsp zest of an organic lemon
3 tbsp clarified unsalted butter

It is best to cook the potatoes the day before. In a pot, bring a generous amount of water and salt to a boil. Cook them for about 20 minutes until they are done. Peel the potatoes and let them cool completely. Put the quark in a bowl. Put the potatoes through a potato ricer, grate them finely, or mash them with a fork. Add the potatoes, flour, sugar, and egg to the quark or yogurt and combine everything into a smooth dough. Season to taste with the salt, nutmeg, and lemon zest. Let the dough rest, uncovered, for 30 minutes.

Heat the clarified butter in a large, heavy, frying pan. For each cake, cut off 1 tablespoon of dough and in place it in the hot butter. Flatten it gently and form it into the shape of a drop. Cook each side over moderate heat for about 3 minutes until they are golden-brown. Serve immediately.

TIP A freshly-brewed cup of coffee is just the thing to go with these freshly-made potato cakes. They also taste good if you add a handful of currants or raisins to the dough. Just reduce the amount of sugar by 2 tablespoons.

Westfalian Quark Surprise

My colleague Jan Bockholt often sang the praises of this delicious layered dessert with caramelized crumbled pumpernickel. We got the recipe from his mother Ria who told us Jan adored this dessert even as a little boy. During the two years he spent in Canada, Jan whipped up this dessert to combat homesickness and to bring to parties, where it was a great success. Since then, Westfalian Quark Surprise must have become well-known in several parts of Canada since every second party guest eagerly asked Jan for the recipe.   Birgit

Serves 4

12⅓ oz (350g) sour cherries from a jar
7½oz (200g) pumpernickel bread
3 tbsp unsalted butter
8 tbsp sugar
1 cup heavy cream
1lb 2oz (500g) quark (alternatively, use a thick and creamy, plain, non-fat yogurt
1 tsp pure vanilla extract

Drain the cherries in a sieve. Crumble the pumpernickel finely. Melt the butter in a frying pan and add the 4 tablespoons of sugar. Stirring constantly over moderate heat, caramelize the sugar. Add the crumbled pumpernickel to the caramel and combine everything together well. Set on one side. In a bowl, beat the cream until it forms stiff peaks. In a second bowl, mix together the quark or yogurt, the vanilla extract, and the rest of the sugar. Gently fold the whipped cream into the quark or yogurt mixture.

Layer the ingredients in a glass bowl or in four individual glass dessert bowls. First, make a layer of quark or yogurt and whipped cream, next, a layer of well-drained cherries and then a layer of crumbled pumpernickel. Repeat until you have 6 layers. Chill in the refrigerator for 1–2 hours.

TIP This also tastes good made with whole cranberries from a jar instead of sour cherries.

Cakes & Cookies

Strawberry Cheesecake

My mother makes this cheesecake using an old family recipe. It is as filling as a regular cheesecake but more refreshing. At some point, she had the brilliant idea of crowning the cake with fresh strawberries. This special cheesecake has been the star of every festive tea party ever since. Birgit

Makes 1
10-in (26-cm) cake

4 tbsp sugar
1 large egg
5½oz (150g) flour
1 level tsp baking powder
1 pinch of salt
4 tbsp cold unsalted butter
2 cups milk
1½–2 packages of vanilla pudding mix (not instant)
1 cup sugar
1¾lb (800g) sour cream
1 tbsp cornstarch
2.2lb (1kg) strawberries, the same size, if possible
5½oz (150g) raspberry jam

Cream together the sugar and egg in a bowl. Add the flour, baking powder, and salt and mix well. Add the cold butter. Using your hands, and working quickly, knead the ingredients to form a dough. Shape the dough into a ball, wrap it in plastic wrap, and chill in the refrigerator for at least 1 hour. Measure out enough pudding mix for 4 cups of milk. Measure out 12 tablespoons of the milk and put it in a small bowl. Stir the pudding mix and sugar into the cold milk until there are no more lumps. In a pot, bring the rest of the milk to a boil, remove it from the heat, and mix in the pudding mixture using a wire whisk. Return the pot to the heat and, stirring constantly, cook the pudding for about 1 minute until it thickens. Remove it from the heat.

Place the sour cream in a mixing bowl. Stir in the cooled pudding until the mixture is smooth, then stir in the cornstarch. Preheat the oven to 400°F (200°C). Butter a 10-in (26-cm) spring-form pan. Roll out the pastry to line the base and make an edge about 1in (2½cm) high. Lay it into the pan and press it down firmly with your fingers.

Spread the filling evenly over the pastry base. Place the pan on the bottom rack of the preheated oven and bake the cheesecake for about 45 minutes until it is just lightly browned. If it starts to brown too quickly, cover it with aluminum foil. Remove the cheesecake from the oven, take it out of the pan, and set it on a cake rack to cool. Then put it in the refrigerator to chill for at least 2 hours. Wash the strawberries and pat them dry. Cut off the stems horizontally so that the berries stand upright. Arrange the strawberries in circles on the cheesecake. Heat the jam in a small pot and push it through a fine sieve. Glaze the strawberries with the hot strawberry jam.

Recipe photo on page 130

Rhubarb-Meringue Cake

Buttery-light cake, pieces of juicy rhubarb, and a light-and-airy meringue topping make this cake irresistible. This is a recipe of Aunt Emilie's. Ever since I can remember, she baked this cake every spring as soon as the first rhubarb was ripe in the garden. Especially when Matthias came to visit from Vancouver, rhubarb cake absolutely had to be on the table. Because it isn't made in Canada, at least, not yet! Birgit

**Makes 1
10-in (26-cm) cake**
2.2lb (1kg) rhubarb
9oz (250g) unsalted butter, at room temperature
3½oz (100g) sugar
1 tsp pure vanilla extract
1 pinch of salt
1 extra-large egg
9oz (250g) flour
2½ tsp baking powder
3 cold egg whites
1 pinch of salt
3½oz (100g) superfine sugar

Wash the rhubarb and cut the stalks into about 1½-in (4-cm) long pieces. Pull off the string and put the rhubarb on one side. Preheat the oven to 375 °F (190 °C) or 350 °F (180 °C) if you are using convection heat. Butter a 10-in (26-cm) spring-form pan, dust it lightly with flour, and shake out the excess flour.

To make the cake, in a bowl, cream together the butter and sugar. Mix in the vanilla extract, salt, and egg. Mix the flour and the baking powder together and add them to the butter and egg mixture to make a batter. Pour the batter into the spring-form pan. Spread it smooth with a spatula. Cover the batter with the pieces of rhubarb and lightly press them in.

Place the cake on the middle rack of the preheated oven and bake it for 35–40 minutes. Test the cake to see if it is done (*see* tip on page 146). Remove the cake from the oven but don't turn off the oven yet.

To make the meringue topping, in a pre-chilled bowl, quickly whip the egg whites with 1 pinch of salt until they form stiff peaks. Gradually whisk in the sugar. Spread the meringue on top of the cake, return it to the oven and bake it for about 8 minutes until the meringue is lightly browned. Check the cake now and then to make sure the meringue does not become too dark.

Recipe photo on page 131

TIP This cake tastes very good in summer, too. Just use red currants instead of rhubarb. The red currants can be stripped from their stems easily with a fork.

Zwetschgendatschi (Plum Tart)

Tarts made with yeast dough baked on a baking tray are wonderful, especially when topped with sweet, fully-ripe, plums or prunes. Each area of Germany has its very own special plum tart recipe. Ours is from the south, where it is known as "Zwetschgendatschi." Since the tart calls for a great deal of prepared fruit, I had to help out even as a young child. So I well know that you have to cut the plums or prunes so they hang together accordion style. And you have to closely pack the plums in rows, just like the packed rows in the economy section of an airplane, where everyone has their seat pushed back as far as it will go. Birgit

Makes 1 baking tray

1lb 2oz (500g) flour
1½oz (42g) yeast cake or
2 tsp active dry yeast
3½oz (100g) sugar
1 cup lukewarm milk
4½oz (125g) softened
unsalted butter
2 large eggs
1 pinch of salt
2.2lb (2kg) fresh plums
or prunes
1¾oz (50g) sugar

Sift the flour into a bowl and make a deep well in the center. Crumble the yeast in the well, then add the sugar and 4 tablespoons of the milk. Stirring in the well, carefully incorporate a bit of flour into the liquid. Cover the bowl and leave it in a warm place for 20 minutes until the yeast bubbles up.

Melt the butter. Add the rest of the milk and sugar, the eggs, butter, and salt to the dough. Using your hands, knead the dough until it no longer sticks to your fingers. This takes about 3–4 minutes. Cover and let the dough rise in a warm place for 40 minutes more until it has almost doubled in volume.

Wash the plums or prunes, and cut them in half, but not completely, so that the halves are still attached together. Remove the pits. Then cut each half lengthwise into two, again not completely, so that the fruit hangs together like an accordion. Grease a 16×12×1in (40×30×2.5cm) baking tray or line it with parchment paper.

Turn out the dough onto a floured work surface, roll it out into a rectangle the size of the baking tray, and place it on the baking tray. Using the tines of a fork, prick the dough all over. Arrange the plums or prunes in closely-packed rows on top of the dough. Cover the tart with a cloth, and let it rise for 20 minutes more. Preheat the oven to 400°F (200°C). Place the baking tray on the middle rack of the oven and bake the tart for 30 minutes. Remove it from the oven and sprinkle it with the sugar while it is still hot.

Raspberry Sponge Roll

In Aunt Emilie's garden there are two giant raspberry bushes. One of them is very old. The fruit of the younger bush tastes very good but when compared with the intense taste of the berries from the older bush they are worlds apart. Emilie has been baking this raspberry sponge roll for me since I can remember. Would another type of birthday cake do? Unthinkable!

Birgit

Makes 1 sponge roll

4 large eggs
4 tbsp hot water
5½oz (150g) sugar
1 tsp pure vanilla extract
2½oz (75g) flour
1¾oz (50g) cornstarch
¾ tsp double-acting baking powder
3½oz (100g) sliced almonds
1 tsp unsalted butter
1¼ cups heavy cream
1 tbsp confectioner's sugar
10½oz (300g) raspberries

Line a 16×12×1in (40×30×2.5cm) baking tray with parchment paper. Preheat the oven to 400°F (200°C) or 350°F (180°C) on the convection setting. Using the highest setting of an electric hand mixer, beat the eggs and the 4 tablespoons of hot water in a large bowl until thick and foamy. Gradually add the sugar (reserving 3 teaspoons for later) and the vanilla extract. Beat for 2 minutes more. Combine the flour, cornstarch and baking powder, sift over the egg mixture, and gently fold them in. Pour the sponge batter onto the lined baking tray. It should be about ⅓in (1cm) deep.

Place the tray on the bottom rack of the oven and bake the sponge for 10–15 minutes. Lightly sprinkle 1 tablespoon sugar on a clean dish towel. Remove the baked sponge from the oven and turn it out immediately on to the towel. Quickly, and carefully, peel off the parchment paper. Using the towel, roll up the sponge from the short side and let cool.

Melt the butter in a nonstick frying pan. Add the sliced almonds and lightly roast them, stirring constantly. Sprinkle 1 teaspoon of sugar over them, stir briefly, and remove from the heat. Whip the cream lightly, add the confectioner's sugar, and continue whipping until the cream forms stiff peaks. Unroll the sponge, leaving it on the towel. Spread half of the whipped cream evenly over the sponge. Sprinkle the raspberries with 1 teaspoon of sugar and press them lightly into the cream. Re-roll the sponge and filling but don't roll it up too firmly otherwise too much cream will squeeze out from the sides. Slice the ends of the roll with a knife to make them even. Spread the remaining cream over the raspberry roll and sprinkle it with the roasted sliced almonds.

TIP Sliced almonds often keep getting darker after roasting so as soon as you have roasted them, turn them out of the frying pan on to a cold plate.

Gugelhupf

When I bake this delicious molded cake with my two sons, I always use the old glazed-pottery mold I inherited from my family. Gugelhupfs, and only gugelhupfs, have been baked in this mold for a century. Even older is this gugelhupf recipe with yeast, which tastes so much better than recipes calling for sponge cake batter with baking powder added. Try out this version and see what you think!   Linn

**Makes 1
9½-in (24-cm)
Gugelhupf**

*3½oz (100g) raisins
3½oz (100g) currants
14oz (400g) all-purpose flour
1oz (30g) yeast cake or
¾ tsp active dry yeast
½ cup (130g) sugar
⅓ cup lukewarm milk
9oz (250g) unsalted butter
1 tsp pure vanilla extract
4 large eggs
1 pinch of salt
zest of 1 organic lemon
3 tbsp confectioner's sugar*

Wash the raisins and currants in hot water and put them on paper towels to drain. Set 2 tablespoons of the flour on one side. Sift the remaining flour into a bowl and make a deep well in the center. Crumble the yeast in the well, then add the sugar and 4 tablespoons of the milk. Stirring in the well, carefully incorporate a bit of flour into the liquid. Cover the bowl and leave it in a warm place for 20 minutes until the yeast bubbles up.

Set aside 1 tablespoon of the butter. Melt the rest of the butter in a pot. Using the dough attachment of an electric mixer, mix the melted butter, remaining sugar, vanilla extract, remaining milk, eggs, salt, and lemon zest into the dough until it shows bubbles. Toss the raisins and currants in the remaining 2 tablespoons of flour and gently fold them in to the dough. Grease a 9½in (24cm) gugelhupf mold (or a fluted tube pan), place the dough in it, cover it with plastic wrap, and let it rise in a warm place for 40 minutes.

Preheat the oven to 350°F (180°C). Place the gugelhupf on the middle rack of the oven and bake it for about 50–60 minutes. Test the cake to see if it is done (*see* tip page 146). Remove the gugelhupf from the oven and cool for about 20 minutes. Turn the cake out on to a cake rack. Melt the reserved 1 tablespoon of butter and brush it over the cake. Sprinkle the cake with the confectioner's sugar.

TIP This cake doesn't just go beautifully with coffee, tea, or cocoa, but also tastes fabulous with a glass of red wine or a sweet dessert wine, such as ice wine or port. If you like, you can use candied lemon or orange peel instead of or along with the currants, adjusting the measurements accordingly.

Butter-Almond Squares

These aren't classic butter squares made with a yeast dough but amazingly moist non-yeast butter squares topped with almonds that are quickly made. My grandmother's recipe is particularly well suited for inexperienced bakers because this isn't simply one of the best cakes in the world, but also one of the easiest to make.   Linn

Makes 1 baking tray

For the dough:

1 cup heavy cream
1 cup sugar
1 tsp pure vanilla extract
1 pinch of salt
4 large eggs
2 cups all-purpose flour
½ tsp double-acting baking powder

For the topping:

8 tbsp unsalted butter
½ cup sugar
4 tbsp heavy cream
1 cup sliced almonds

Preheat the oven to 350°F (180°C). Line a 16×12in (40×30cm) baking tray that is at least ½in (1½cm) deep with parchment paper. To make the dough for the base, in a mixing bowl, beat the cream, sugar, vanilla extract, salt, and eggs with an electric hand mixer until thick and fluffy. Sift in the flour and baking powder and keep beating until the dough blisters. Spread out the dough on the parchment paper. Place the baking tray on the middle rack of the oven and prebake the base for 10–20 minutes, until it is lightly browned.

While the base is baking, prepare the topping. In a pot, melt the butter over low heat. Remove it from the heat and let it cool for about 5 minutes. Beat in the sugar and cream then add the sliced almonds. Remove the partially-baked base from the oven and, using a spatula, carefully spread the topping over the it. Be careful that you don't tear the base! Return the baking tray to the oven and bake the cake for 15 minutes more.

Custard-Cream Squares

There are probably as many recipes for "Eierschecke" as there are Saxon families. The variations are endless. Our recipe is a classic made with yeast dough, quark or yogurt, and custard.

Makes 1 baking tray

For the dough:

12oz (350g) all-purpose flour

¾ tsp instant active dry yeast

½ cup milk

3 tbsp sugar

3 tbsp unsalted butter

1 large egg

1 pinch of salt

For the quark or yogurt topping:

2 large eggs

5 tbsp sugar

1lb 2oz (500g) quark (alternatively, use thick and creamy, plain, non-fat yogurt)

1–2 packages vanilla pudding mix (not instant)

zest of ½ organic orange

For the egg custard topping:

1–2 packages vanilla pudding mix (not instant)

2 cups milk

6oz (175g) unsalted butter, cut into small pieces

3 large eggs

1 pinch of salt

To make the dough, sift the flour into a bowl and mix in the dry yeast. Heat the milk until it is lukewarm and pour it into a large mixing bowl. Add the sugar, butter, egg, and 1 pinch of salt and combine everything using the dough hook of an electric mixer. Then, using your hands, knead the dough until it no longer sticks to your hands. Cover the dough. Let it rise in a warm place for 30–40 minutes until it has almost doubled in volume. Line a 16×12×1in (40×30×2.5cm) baking tray with parchment paper. Roll out the dough to fit the tray and place it on the parchment paper. Shape an edge, re-cover the dough and let it rise in a warm place for 15–20 minutes.

To make the quark or yogurt topping, first measure out enough pudding mix for 2 cups of milk. Beat the eggs and sugar together until fluffy. Mix in the quark or yogurt, the pudding mix, and the orange zest. To make the custard, preheat the oven to 350°F (180°C). Measure out ⅓ more pudding mix than the instructions require for 2 cups of milk. Cook the pudding mix according to package directions with the 2 cups of milk. Pour the pudding into a large bowl. Using a wire whisk, beat the butter and sugar into the hot mixture. Let the mixture cool until it is lukewarm. Separate the eggs. Whisk the yolks into the cooled pudding well. Beat the egg whites with a pinch of salt until they form stiff peaks. Fold them into the pudding. Spread the quark or yogurt topping over the dough, then spread the custard layer. Place the baking tray on the middle rack of the oven and bake for 40 minutes until the top layer is golden-brown. After 15–20 minutes, cover with parchment paper so that the top layer doesn't become too dark. Remove from the oven, let cool, and cut into squares.

Potato and Jam Pastries

These pastries are not only well-suited to elegant birthday parties, they are a delicacy you can serve any day. Not overly sweet, they are ideal for breakfast or a coffee break on a normal week day, which is exactly when my mother so often used to serve them.   Birgit

Makes 1 dozen pastries

9oz (250g) salad potatoes, such as Yukon Gold
1¾oz (50g) softened unsalted butter
2 large eggs
3½oz (100g) sugar
9oz (250g) flour
½ tsp double-acting baking powder
1 pinch of salt
1 tsp pure vanilla extract
12 heaping tsp jam to taste
3 tbsp milk
a bit of confectioner's sugar

The day before you want to make the pastries, boil the unpeeled potatoes in liberally salted water until they are done. On baking day, peel the potatoes and put them through a potato ricer. Cream the softened butter and the eggs and sugar in a bowl until thick and fluffy. Mix in the vanilla extract and the potatoes. Mix the flour with the baking powder and salt and beat into the potato mixture. Lightly knead the dough, gather it into a ball, cover it with plastic wrap, and let it rest for 1½ hours in the refrigerator.

Preheat the oven to 400°F (200°C). Line a baking tray with parchment paper. Roll out the dough on a floured work surface until it is ¼in (5mm) thick. Cut out 12 squares about 4in (10cm) on each side. Spread each square with 1 heaping teaspoon of the jam. Working from the tip, roll up the squares diagonally into croissant shapes. Place them on the parchment paper and brush them with milk. Place the baking tray on the middle rack of the oven and bake the triangles for 20–25 minutes until they are golden-brown. Remove the baking tray from the oven and dust the pastries lightly with confectioner's sugar.

TIP Apricot jam, plum butter, or rosehip butter also make good fillings for the pastries. Don't worry if a bit of the jam leaks out when the pastries are baking, they taste even better.

Lemon Cake

Why does this cake taste so amazingly moist? The secret is really simple — it is baked for a long time at a low temperature! This is an excellent cake to serve in summer and a great alternative to fruit tarts.

Makes 1 cake

Batter:

10½oz (300g) softened unsalted butter
10½oz (300g) sugar
5 large eggs
10½oz (300g) flour
¼ tsp double-acting baking powder
1 pinch of salt
juice and zest of 1 organic lemon

Glaze:

juice of ½ lemon
1 cup confectioner's sugar

Preheat the oven to 275°F (140°C). Butter a 12×4½in (30×11cm) loaf pan. To make the batter, in a large bowl, cream the butter and sugar together until fluffy using an electric hand mixer and gradually add the eggs. Sift the flour, and baking powder into the mixture. Add the salt, lemon juice, and lemon peel and beat on the highest speed until the batter forms bubbles. Pour the batter into the loaf pan and bake the cake on the middle rack of the oven for about 90 minutes.

When the cake is nicely browned on top, test it with a toothpick or wooden skewer to see if it is done (see below). Remove the cake from the oven and let it cool down a bit. Turn out the cake and put it on a cake platter. To make the glaze, slowly pour the lemon juice into the confectioner's sugar and stir it until the glaze is completely smooth. Spread the glaze over the lemon cake.

TIP Lemon cake freezes very well and tastes as though it were freshly baked after defrosting!

To test if a cake is done, insert a wooden toothpick or skewer into the center of the cake. If the toothpick or skewer come out clean, the cake is done.

Margot Pehrs from Schleswig-Holstein

Cake, Cookies, and a Fresh Breeze

How many cakes does Margot Pehrs of Wedel in Schleswig-Holstein bake each week? "At least one," she says and then, thinking it over, says "but it might also be as many as three a day." The cakes are much appreciated by her family, friends, and neighbors. She is even happy to bake to order, for example, for a grandchild who wants to take a butter cake to work. At the top of Margot's baking hit list are sponge cakes such as lemon cake, butter cake, and poppyseed cake with streusel. She also always bakes enough sand cookies in advance so that the large cookie jar on the bottom shelf of the cupboard is never empty. She probably has no time left for other hobbies? She laughs again heartily and her eyes sparkle as she tells us how often she is underway. Yesterday she was at a ball until 3 o'clock in the morning, soon she will be leaving on one of her many trips, then

there's gardening and there's knitting. In fact, there's always the start of a pullover for one of her four great-grandchildren in the knitting basket, with its many-colored wools, along with a number of socks, those are always needed. She can hardly believe it herself that she's almost 90. After all, Margot still does almost all of her errands by bicycle or on foot. In the town where she lives, a small northern-German town directly on the Elbe river, the distances are not great. From her garden, you can hear the horns of the ships tooting in response as they are greeted at the nearby "Willkomm-Höft." Recently, at a party, she met an acquaintance whom she hadn't seen for 60 years who told her "You still have the same eyes, Margot." Whoever sees her, believes this right away.

Poppyseed Streusel Squares

Margot Pehrs discovered the original recipe in the early 1950s in a magazine and kept amending it until this much-loved poppyseed cake was perfected.   Linn

Makes 1 baking tray

Filling:

9oz (250g) raisins
2 tbsp rum
1lb 2oz (500g) ground poppyseed
2 cups milk
2½oz (70g) semolina
5½oz (150g) sugar
1 pinch of salt
1 large egg
juice of ½ lemon

Base:

5½oz (150g) softened unsalted butter
5½oz (150g) sugar
2 large eggs
1 pinch of salt
zest of ½ organic lemon
9oz (250g) flour
2 tsp baking powder

Streusel:

7½oz (200g) unsalted butter
9oz (250g) flour
9oz (250g) sugar
1 pinch of salt

To make the filling, soak the raisins in the rum for 30 minutes. Place the poppyseed in a bowl and pour 2 cups of boiling water over it. Stir, and let the poppyseed swell for 15 minutes. In a pot, bring the milk to a boil, and add the semolina, sugar, and salt. Stirring constantly, cook the mixture for 1 minute. Remove it from the heat. Pour the semolina into the poppyseed, stir in the egg and the lemon juice, and let cool. Preheat the oven to 350°F (180°C). Line a 16×12×1in (40×30×2.5cm) baking tray with parchment paper.

To make the base, using an electric hand mixer cream together the butter and sugar. Gradually add the eggs, salt, lemon peel, flour, and baking powder. Mix everything together until the dough is smooth. Spread out the dough on the parchment paper.

To make the streusel, first melt the butter. Put the flour, sugar, and salt in a bowl, add the melted butter, and mix until large crumbs (the streusel) form. Spread the poppyseed filling over the dough. Evenly sprinkle the streusel over the filling. Place the baking tray on the middle rack of the oven and bake the poppyseed squares for 40–45 minutes.

Margot Pehrs from Schleswig-Holstein

150

Quark Stollen

A German Christmas is unthinkable without stollen. This version is made with an especially light quark-and-yeast dough, and is therefore not as heavy as a bona fide Dresden stollen. It also tastes good all year round at Sunday breakfast—in fact, it tastes especially good with the strawberry and rhubarb jam on page 170.

Makes 1 stollen

1lb 2oz (500g) flour
1½oz (42g) yeast cake or
2 tsp active dry yeast
7½oz (200g) sugar
½ cup lukewarm milk
5½oz (150g) raisins
9oz (250g) quark
(alternatively, use thick
and creamy, plain,
non-fat yogurt)
2 large eggs
7 tbsp softened unsalted
butter
1 pinch of salt
1oz (25g) candied lemon
peel
1oz (25g) candied orange
peel
1 tsp melted unsalted butter
3 tbsp confectioner's sugar

Sift the flour into a bowl and make a deep well in the center. Crumble the yeast in the well, then add the sugar and 4 tablespoons of the milk. Stirring in the well, carefully incorporate a bit of flour into the liquid. Cover the bowl and leave it in a warm place for 20 minutes until the yeast bubbles up.

Wash the raisins in hot water and drain them. Add the raisins, the remaining milk, quark or yogurt, eggs, butter, the remaining sugar, salt, candied lemon peel, and candied orange peel to the dough. Using the dough hook of a hand mixer, knead the dough until it no longer sticks to the side of the bowl.

Line a baking tray with parchment paper. Flour your hands and gather the dough into a long loaf, place it on the baking tray, and place the stollen on the middle rack of a cold oven.

Heat the oven to 350°F (180°C) and bake the stollen for 45–55 minutes. After about 15–20 minutes, when the stollen is already light brown, it is important to cover it with parchment paper, otherwise it will become too dark. Remove the stollen from the oven and brush melted butter over it immediately. Let it cool. Before serving, dust the stollen with sifted confectioner's sugar.

TIP All the ingredients should be at room temperature so make sure to take them out of the refrigerator in advance. There are many ways to vary this stollen recipe. You can leave out the candied lemon peel and, instead, use grated organic lemon peel, or add chopped almonds or pistachios to the dough or put marzipan paste in the middle of the dough.

Classic Cheesecake

No birthday, christening, or wedding day is complete without cheesecake and there are many different versions. They can be made with raisins, with mandarin segments, or as a creamy torte. The one thing they do have in common is that they all taste wonderful. This classic version is quickly made, uncomplicated, yet still very tasty and creamy.

**Makes 1
9½-in (24-cm) cake**

For the crust:

*9oz (250g) flour
4½oz (125g) cold unsalted butter, cut into pieces
3 tbsp sugar
1 pinch of salt
1 large egg*

For the filling:

*6oz (170g) ricotta cheese
1lb (450g) cream cheese
½ cup sour cream
1 tsp pure vanilla extract
4½oz (130g) sugar
4 large eggs
¼ cup cornstarch
4½oz (125g) melted unsalted butter
zest of 1 organic lemon*

Sift the flour into a bowl. Add the butter, sugar, salt, and egg. Using your hands, and working quickly, knead the mixture to form a smooth, elastic, dough. Shape the dough into a ball, wrap it in plastic wrap, and put it in the refrigerator to rest for at least 30 minutes.

Preheat the oven to 350°F (180°C) and place the oven rack on the second level from the bottom. Butter a 9½-in (24-cm) spring-form pan. Place the ricotta cheese in a fine sieve and place the sieve over a bowl. Let the ricotta drain for at least two hours. In a bowl, using an electric hand mixer, blend together the ricotta, cream cheese, and the sour cream until there are no lumps. Add the vanilla extract, sugar, eggs, cornstarch, melted butter, and lemon peel.

Roll out the short crust pastry to line the base and sides of the spring-form pan. Pour in the filling. Place the pan on the rack and bake the cake for about 45–55 minutes.

TIP If the cheesecake starts to brown too quickly when it is baking, simply cover it with parchment paper. This recipe is the basic cheesecake recipe and it can be varied quite easily. Blackberries or red currants taste delicious in the filling, as of course do raisins or pieces of apple.

Braided Sunday Loaf

Nothing in the world tastes better on a rainy Sunday morning than a freshly-baked yeast loaf with butter and strawberry jam! By the way, the fresher the yeast (if you buy cakes of yeast), the better the dough will rise. Don't buy yeast of any kind that only has a few days left before its "best before" date! Linn

Makes 1 braided loaf

2.2lb (1kg) flour
1½oz (42g) yeast cake or
2 tsp active dry yeast
4oz (110g) sugar
1 cup lukewarm milk
4¼oz (120g) softened unsalted butter
3 large eggs
1 pinch of salt
1 tsp pure vanilla extract
1 egg yolk
crystallized sugar as needed or ¼ cup chopped almonds

Sift the flour into a bowl and make a deep well in the center. Crumble the yeast in the well, then add the sugar and 4 tablespoons of the milk. Stirring in the well, carefully incorporate a bit of flour into the liquid. Cover the bowl and leave it in a warm place for 20 minutes until the yeast bubbles up. Knead the remaining sugar, the remaining milk, the butter, eggs, salt, and vanilla extract into the dough.

Using your hands, knead the dough until it no longer sticks to your fingers, which takes about 3–4 minutes. Gather the dough into a ball, place it in a bowl, and cover it. Let it rise in a warm place for 40 minutes until it has almost doubled in volume.

Preheat the oven to 350 °F (180 °C) or 325 °F (170 °C) on the convection setting. Line a baking tray with parchment paper. Divide the dough into three equal pieces and roll them on the parchment paper into three long ropes. Starting from the middle rope, braid the ropes. Beat the egg yolk, brush it over the braided loaf, and sprinkle the loaf with crystallized sugar or chopped almonds. Place the baking tray on the middle rack of the oven and bake the loaf for 35–45 minutes. After about 20–25 minutes, cover it with parchment paper so that it does not become too brown. After 35 minutes, rap the loaf with a finger knuckle; if it sounds hollow, the loaf is done!

TIP At Easter-time, this braided loaf can quickly be turned into an attractive Easter wreath loaf. Just attach the braid ends to each other to form a round wreath. Place an unshelled, dyed, hard-boiled, egg in the center, brush the wreath with egg yolk and bake as above.

Baked Apple Cake

Without exaggeration, this baked apple cake is one of the best cakes in the world. It is incomparable, with its creamy rich vanilla taste, which contrasts beautifully with the wonderful tartness of the apples! Add a cup of hot coffee and all is right with the world.   Linn

**Makes 1
9½-in (24-cm) cake**

For the pastry:

7½oz (200g) all-purpose flour
½ tsp baking powder
5 tbsp sugar
1 tsp pure vanilla extract
1 pinch of salt
1 large egg
7 tbsp softened unsalted butter

For the custard filling:

8 small, tart apples
juice of 1 lemon
vanilla pudding mix (not instant)
3 tbsp sugar
2½ cups heavy cream
3 tbsp sliced almonds

Preheat the oven to 350 °F (180 °C) or 325 °F (170 °C) if you are using convection heat. Grease a 9½-in (24-cm) spring-form pan. To make the pastry, sift the flour and baking powder into a bowl. Using the dough hook attachment, knead the sugar, vanilla extract, salt, egg, and butter in an electric mixer to form a dough. Gather the dough into a smooth ball and divide it in two. Roll out one ball to line the base of the spring-form pan. Wrap the remaining dough in plastic wrap and chill. Lay the pastry in the base and prick it with the tines of a fork. Place the pan on the middle rack of the oven and prebake the base for about 15 minutes. Remove from the oven and let cool for 15 minutes. Leave the oven on.

Form the second ball of dough into a long roll and shape it into an edge for the cake. Peel the whole apples and remove the cores with an apple corer. Sprinkle them with lemon juice and set them upright on the pastry base. Measure out enough pudding mix for 2 cups of milk in a bowl. Stir in the sugar and 1 cup of the cream. In a pot, bring the remaining cream to a boil, stirring constantly. Remove the cream from the stove and, stirring constantly with a wire whisk, pour in the pudding mixture. Return the pot to the stove and let the custard cook for 2 minutes more. Pour the hot custard over the apples and sprinkle the sliced almonds over the top. Place the cake on the middle rack of the oven and bake it for 65 minutes.

TIP If you would like to bake the cake with raisins, soak 5 tablespoons of raisins in 2–3 tablespoons rum for 30 minutes, sprinkle them over the apples, and then pour the custard over the apples.

Kalter Hund (Cold Dog)

This cake with an odd name has the advantage of not needing to be baked and the disadvantage (for some) of being high in calories. But it tastes wonderfully of melt-in-your mouth chocolate and evokes memories of joyous children's birthday parties and game such as pass-the-parcel and egg-and-spoon races. Also, it is a great dessert for a larger group since it serves at least 8 !

Makes 1 cake

1lb (450g) milk chocolate couverture (baking chocolate)

5½oz (150g) dark chocolate couverture (baking chocolate)

5½oz (150g) coconut cream

1 cup heavy cream

about 9oz (250g) crunchy butter cookies

Butter a long loaf pan and line it with parchment paper or a freezer bag. Finely chop the chocolate and coconut cream. Put them in a pot and pour in the cream. Stirring constantly over low heat, gently warm the ingredients until the chocolate and coconut cream are melted and smooth. Starting and ending with a layer of chocolate, layer the chocolate mixture and the butter cookies in alternate rows in the pan. Put the cold dog in the refrigerator to harden for at least 5 hours, ideally overnight. The next day, carefully loosen the cold dog from the pan with a knife, turn it out and peel off the parchment paper or plastic.

TIP Cold dog tastes best when it is still a bit cool!

Bear Paw Cookies

These little cookie paws are crispy on the outside and wonderfully soft and chocolatey on the inside. Traditionally, they are considered to be Christmas cookies, but there's no reason not to eat them throughout the winter.

Makes 4 dozen cookies
6 egg whites
1lb 2oz (500g) sugar
7½oz (200g) grated dark chocolate
1 tsp cinnamon
zest of ½ organic lemon
1lb 2oz (500g) ground hazelnuts
1 tbsp cocoa
sugar to taste

Beat the egg whites with an electric hand mixer until they form stiff peaks, gradually adding the sugar, and stirring constantly. Mix in the chocolate, cinnamon, lemon peel, hazelnuts, and cocoa. Let the dough rest for 4 hours.

Shape the mixture into walnut-sized balls and roll them in sugar. If you have a wooden bear-paw mold, press the dough into the mold. Alternatively, mold the dough in the hollow of a teaspoon. Place the molded bear paws on a baking tray lined with parchment paper. Leave the bear paws to dry overnight.

The next day, preheat the oven to 265°F (130°C). Place the baking tray on the middle rack of the oven and bake the bear paws for 20 minutes. Turn off the oven and let the bear paws rest in the oven for 5 minutes more. The paws are even more chocolatey when they are dipped in melted chocolate after baking.

TIP How can you use up 6 left over egg yolks? One idea is to just keep on baking since many kinds of cookie recipes, such as those for vanilla crescents or lemon hearts, call for egg yolks only. Further tips can be found in the appendix (page 187).

Heidesand (Sand Cookies)

My grandmother always had sand cookies on hand and always baked a new batch well before the cookie jar was empty. She still always brings a few cookies with her when she comes to visit. I was really surprised to learn how few ingredients are used in the cookie dough, since the cookies taste very sophisticated. The secret is the fact that the butter is melted and browned, and then allowed to resolidify. Linn

Makes about 5 dozen cookies

9½oz (275g) unsalted butter
9oz (250g) sugar
1 tsp pure vanilla extract
13oz (375g) flour
1 tsp baking powder
2 tbsp milk
¼ tsp salt

Over moderate heat, melt the butter in a pot and brown it until it gives off a tantalizing aroma. Remove the butter from the heat, pour it into a mixing bowl and let it cool for about 1 hour until it has hardened. Then, using an electric hand mixer, beat in the sugar and vanilla extract until the mixture is fluffy. As you are mixing, gradually sift the flour into the bowl. Add the baking powder, milk, and salt. Using your hands, knead the dough until all the ingredients are well combined. Shape the dough into rolls about 1-in (3-cm) thick and put them in the refrigerator to chill for at least 2 hours.

Preheat the oven to 350°F (180°C). Line a baking tray with parchment paper. Cut the rolls of dough into rounds about ¼-in (5-mm) thick and place them on the parchment paper. Bake the cookies on the middle rack of the oven for about 15 minutes, until they are just slightly browned. Remove them from the oven and let cool.

TIP Fill the cookie jar with sand cookies—and wait for visitors.
It's important to put a whole cookie in your mouth and let it dissolve!

Marzipan Delights

These exquisite little marzipan balls are a Frankfurt specialty, where they are known as "Bethmännchen." The recipe is said to have originated with the Bethmanns, a renowned Frankfurt banking family. Four almond halves were pressed into the cookie, one for each of the four Bethmann sons. Then a son died, and there were only 3 almond halves.

**Makes about
2 dozen cookies**

1¾oz (50g) whole almonds
7½oz (200g) marzipan paste
3 tsp superfine sugar
2 tbsp rose water
1 egg white

Blanche the almonds by pouring boiling water over them and let them cool down in the water slightly. Remove the almond skins and carefully divide the nuts in two. Put the almond halves to one side. Knead 2 teaspoons of sugar and the rose water into the almond paste. Shape the paste into a roll about 1½-in (4-cm) thick. Cut the roll into about 24 equally-sized pieces and shape each slice into a small ball. Press 3 almond halves into each ball with their tips pointing upward. Place the cookies on a platter and let them dry for 2–3 hours.

Preheat the oven to 250°F (120°C) or 210°F (100°C) if you are using convection heat. Line a baking tray with parchment paper. Stir 1 teaspoon of sugar into the egg white. Brush the cookies with this mixture and place them on the baking tray. Bake the cookies on the middle rack of the oven for 10 minutes until they are just barely light brown. Be careful that they don't become too dark. Remove them from the oven and let them cool on the baking tray.

TIP Marzipan delights taste especially good when they are allowed to mature in a cookie jar for 2 weeks once they have cooled down.

Franconian Butter Cookies

I love to leaf through old cookbooks and found these delicious butter cookies in the yellowed recipe collection of my boyfriend's grandmother. A scrawled note on the recipe reads: "This recipe was passed on to me by an 80-year-old woman from Nuremberg, who, in turn, got it from her grandmother." Linn

**Makes about
5 dozen cookies**

*4½oz (125g) softened
unsalted butter
7 tbsp softened clarified
unsalted butter
7½oz (200g) sugar
1 pinch of salt
1 large egg
1 tbsp arrack
zest of 1 organic lemon
13oz (375g) flour
2 tsp cinnamon*

Using an electric hand mixer, mix the butter, clarified butter, 3½oz (100g) of the sugar, and the salt until the mixture is creamy. Add the egg, arrack, lemon peel, flour, and 1 teaspoon of the cinnamon. Using your hands, knead the dough until it is smooth and shape it into a ball. Wrap the ball in plastic wrap and let chill for about 1 hour in the refrigerator.

Preheat the oven to 350°F (180°C). Grease a baking tray or line it with parchment paper. Turn out the dough on a lightly floured work surface or between two sheets of plastic wrap and roll it out until it is ¼in (5mm) thick. Cut the dough into shapes or simple circles and place them on the baking tray. Bake the cookies on the middle rack of the oven for about 15 minutes until they are lightly browned. Mix the remaining sugar (3½oz/100g) with the remaining cinnamon (1 teaspoon) and dip the cookies on both sides in the cinnamon-sugar while they are still hot.

TIP If you don't like cinnamon, you can substitute 1 tablespoon of cocoa for the cinnamon in the dough mix and dip the cookies after baking in sugar flavored with vanilla.

Jams, Jellies, and Preserves

Strawberry and Rhubarb Jam

My grandmother always saved the jars of store-bought jams and jellies—they were ideal for her homemade versions. It really looked funny when the lids with pictures of gooseberries or apricots on top were opened to suddenly reveal dark-red strawberry or blackberry jam. Today, two-piece snap lids and jars are more commonly used.　　Linn

Makes about 5 jars
8oz (250ml) each
2.2lb (1kg) strawberries
1lb 2oz (500g) rhubarb
1 package light pectin crystals

Wash and trim the strawberries, which should be free of bruises, and rhubarb. Cut the ends off the rhubarb stalks and chop the stalks into small pieces. Hull the strawberries, place them in a large nonreactive pot, and crush them with a potato masher. Add the rhubarb and sugar. Stirring constantly, bring the fruit to a full rolling boil and cook for 5–8 minutes. Use the masher to crush any still-intact pieces of fruit. When the setting point test shows the jam will set (*see tip on page 176*), immediately ladle the jam into sterilized glass jars, leaving a ¼in (5mm) headspace. Cover the jars with sterilized self-sealing lids and jar rings. Fill a boiling-water canner half-full with hot water and heat the water until it is hot but not boiling. Place the jars in the canner, adding more boiling water if needed to ensure the tops of the jars are covered by about 1in (2.5cm) of water. Bring the water to a rolling boil over high heat and boil for 5 minutes. Let the jars cool. The jam will keep for about 12 months in a cool, dark, place.

Recipe photo on page 168

Quince Jelly

Quince jam is made from the whole fruit, jelly from quince juice. For several years, I've made my own jams and jellies and am always astonished how easy it is to make them. Linn

Makes about 5 jars
8oz (250ml) each
2.2lb (1kg) quince
zest of 1 organic lemon
apple juice, as needed
2.2lb (1kg) sugar

Wash the quince and rub them with a cloth to remove the fuzz from the peel. Cut the fruit into small pieces, removing the blossoms and the stems. Place the fruit, 6⅓ cups of water, and the lemon zest in a pot and bring to a boil in a nonreactive pot. Avoid aluminum pots when making jams and preserves, they react with acids found in fruit and vinegar! Cook the fruit, uncovered, over moderate heat for 45 minutes. Remove the pot from the heat and let the fruit cool. Line a large sieve with a clean dish towel and place it over a large bowl. Pour the cooked quince into the sieve. Press down on the fruit with a large spoon to squeeze the juice out of the fruit.

Measure out 4¼ cups of the quince juice. If it is not enough, top it up with apple juice. In a pot, bring the quince juice and the sugar to a boil over moderate heat. While the juice and sugar are cooking, fill a boiling-water canner half-full with water and heat the water to until it is hot but not boiling. Cook the quince juice and the sugar for about 1 hour, stirring occasionally. Do the jam test (*see* tip page 176). Pour the jelly into sterilized jars, leaving a ¼in (5mm) headspace. Cover the jars with sterilized self-sealing lids and jar rings. Place the jars in the canner, adding boiling water if needed to ensure the tops of the jars are covered by about 1in (2.5cm) of water. Bring the water to a rolling boil over high heat and boil for 5 minutes. Let the jars cool. The jelly will keep for about 12 months in a cool, dark, place.

Recipe photo on page 169

TIP The general rule-of-thumb for making jam is 2.2lb (1kg) fruit to 2.2lb (1kg) sugar; for making jelly, 4¼ cups juice to 2.2lb (1kg) sugar. If you want to use pectin crystals or liquid, reduce the amount of sugar and cooking time according to the manufacturer's instructions on the package.

Plum Butter

This plum butter recipe is from my Aunt Inge, who lives in Frankfurt. She harvests and processes so many plums from her garden each year that she knows how to make the best plum butter. She mailed this recipe to me with the remark: "Do not under any circumstances stir the plums while they are cooking, even if you are tempted to do so." And she was right! It's a real ordeal not to stir a pot for two long hours! Linn

Makes about 5 jars 8oz (250ml) each
4½lb (2kg) plums
2.2lb (1kg) sugar
1 pinch ground cinnamon
5 cloves
2 tbsp freshly-squeezed lemon juice

The evening before cooking the plums, pit them, toss them with the sugar, and place them, cut side down, in a wide nonreactive pot. Leave the pot in a cool place overnight. The next day, bring the plums to a boil over high heat and cook them for 3–5 minutes. Then, reduce the heat and gently simmer the plums, covered, for 1–2 hours. Take the cover off the pot during the last 25 minutes. Do not stir.

Fill a boiling-water canner half-full with water and heat the water until it is hot but not boiling. Stir the cinnamon, cloves, and lemon juice into the plums and cook for 10 minutes more. Remove the pot from the heat. Purée the plums using a hand-held blender. Immediately ladle the plum butter into sterilized glass jars, leaving ¼-in (5-mm) headspace. Cover the jars with sterilized self-sealing lids and jar rings. Place the jars in the canner, and add enough boiling water to ensure the tops of the jars are covered by about 1in (2.5cm) of water. Bring the water to a rolling boil over high heat and boil for 5 minutes. Store the jars away from the light. The plum butter will keep for about 12 months.

TIP Plum butter tastes best during the Christmas season, for example, served with stollen (*see* page 153).

Elisabeth Dahlitz from the Spreewald

Happiness in a Jam Jar

"When I was a child, sour cherry was my favorite kind of jam," reminisces Elisabeth Dahlitz. Sitting there, blinking happily in the sun in her large garden in Burg in the Spreewald, she seems like a young girl. In fact, she looks back on a life filled with work—on her parents' farm, in an office, then as a mother of four.

She has made jams and jellies ever since she can remember. Everything she needs grows in the large farmer's garden behind the house, with its many fruits and vegetables. And there are the medlars, wild plums, and rosehip bushes that grow in the fairy-tale-like Spreewald wetlands. Today, she could simply sit and do nothing; instead, she has returned to working life. Along with her daughter Andrea Veltjens, she runs "Rosenrot & Feengrün," a small, gourmet jam-making business. Elisabeth brings all her experience in jam- and jelly-making to this enterprise, working through mountains of fruit, puréeing and weighing them, and cooking up a storm in the compact kitchen.

"We started off very small," she tells us, "with fruits from our garden and wild plums and rosehips. Now we have to buy extra fruit—but only from locals we know." Elisabeth has revealed her rosehip and orange jam recipe to us.

But just cooking jams isn't enough for Elisabeth. Recently, she and her husband celebrated their golden anniversary and she made all the cakes and food for the party herself. "One has to stay in practice otherwise one forgets everything. In any case, the time to stop will come of its accord." But, for her, this will certainly not be very soon!

Rosehip and Orange Jam

Since you can't buy fresh rosehips in stores, you have to gather them yourself. Granted, the work is a bit arduous and thick garden gloves are a must. But it's worth it, because this jam is something special. This recipe is based on an old family recipe provided by Elisabeth Dahlitz. In the past, only rosehips and a large quantity of sugar were used to make the jam. Today, less sugar is used and orange juice is added which intensifies the flavor of the jam and gives it a fresher, fruitier, taste.

**Makes about 5 jars
8oz (250ml) each**
*4½lb (2kg) rosehips
7fl oz (200ml) freshly-
squeezed orange juice
2.2lb (1kg) sugar*

Gather fully ripe and red rosehips from rose bushes that have not been treated with insecticides. Clean and rinse them. Place them in a large nonreactive pot with cold water, bring them to a boil, and simmer until tender. This takes about 15–20 minutes. Fill a boiling-water canner half-full with water and heat the water until it is hot but not boiling. Drain the rosehips and scrape them through a very fine sieve.

Weigh out 1¾lb (800g) of the rosehip purée and pour it into an enamel or stainless steel pot (avoid aluminum pots when making jams and preserves, they react with acids found in fruit and vinegar!). Add the orange juice and sugar. Bring everything to a full rolling boil and cook for 10 minutes, stirring often. Ladle the jam immediately into sterilized glass jars, leaving a ¼-in (5-mm) headspace. Seal the jars with sterilized self-sealing lids and jar rings or rubber rings. Place the jars on the rack of the boiling-water canner so that they are close but do not touch each other. As needed, add boiling water to ensure the tops of the jars are covered by about 1in (2.5cm) of water. Bring the water to a rolling boil over a high heat and boil for 5 minutes.

TIP Test for the setting point by spreading a bit of hot fruit onto a small, chilled, plate. If it sets, the jam is ready to be filled into jars. If it does not, keep boiling the fruit, testing often to see if it has reached the setting point.

Elisabeth Dahlitz from the Spreewald

Hagebutte & Orange
Hagebutte & Orange
Hagebutte & Orange
Hagebutte & Orange

Pickled Red Cabbage Salad

This recipe comes from a elderly Swiss woman. My friend Sabine lived in Zürich for several years. One day, a neighbor knocked on her door. She had locked herself out and was in her dressing gown! Sabine made her a cup of coffee, consoled her, and called the locksmith. As a thank-you, she received a jar of this red cabbage salad. And later, after asking about it enthusiastically, she was also given the recipe.   Birgit

Makes about 4 jars
2 cups (500ml) each

1 head of red cabbage (about 4½lb (2kg))

3 tbsp salt

8½ cups fruit vinegar (such as apple vinegar)

5 tbsp sugar

1 tbsp coarsely crushed black peppercorns

1 tbsp coarsely crushed allspice berries

a 2in (5cm) strip of thinly-peeled organic orange peel

Quarter the red cabbage and remove its core. Shred the cabbage finely and place it in a glass or ceramic bowl. Add the salt and toss well. Using a cabbage or potato masher, vigorously mash the cabbage for 5 minutes. Place it uncovered in the refrigerator or another cool place for 24 hours. Pour the cabbage into a sieve and let it drain well. Then, place the cabbage and the remaining ingredients in a nonreactive pot. Bring everything to a boil and cook gently over moderate heat for about 15 minutes, stirring often.

Fill a boiling-water canner half-full with water and heat the water until it is hot but not boiling. Using a slotted spoon, remove the cabbage from the pot and fill it into sterilized jars. Return the liquid in the pot to a boil and pour the piping-hot liquid over the red cabbage until the jars are filled, leaving a ¼in (5mm) headspace. Seal the jars with sterilized self-sealing lids and jar rings. Place them in the boiling-water canner, adding boiling water if needed to ensure the tops of the jars are covered by about 1in (2.5cm) of water. Bring the water to a rolling boil over high heat and boil for 10 minutes. Let the cabbage marinate in the jars for at least 1–2 weeks. Stored in a cool, dark, place, the pickled red cabbage will keep for 4–6 months. Store opened jars in the refrigerator and use the red cabbage salad within 3 days.

TIP To make green cabbage salad, replace the allspice berries with caraway seeds and use a bay leaf instead of orange peel.

Sauerkraut

Sauerkraut is best made in a special stoneware sauerkraut pot with a deep indented rim. Once the lid is set on the pot and the rim is filled with water, an air-tight seal is formed but the gases produced by the fermenting process still can escape.

Makes 10½ qts (10l)
11lb (5kg) green cabbage
1½oz (40g) salt (not sea salt)
20 dried juniper berries
1 cup white wine or whey

Remove the outer leaves from the heads of cabbage and set them aside. Quarter the cabbages, core them, and finely shred the cabbage using a cabbage grater or pickling grater. Place half of the outer cabbage leaves on the bottom of the fermenting pot. Place the cabbage in the pot in layers about 4-in (10-cm) high. Salt each layer, add a few juniper berries, and then pound the layer vigorously with a cabbage masher to release as much juice as possible. Only then proceed to make the next layer. Repeat this step until all the cabbage and salt have been used. The pot should be about three-quarters full.

Pour the white wine or whey into the stoneware pot to start the fermenting process. Use the remaining outer leaves of the cabbage to cover the top layer. Fill the rim of the stoneware pot with water and set the lid on top. Let the cabbage ferment at room temperature. An occasional bubbling shows that the fermented process is underway. Check the sauerkraut pot regularly to make sure there is enough liquid since the sauerkraut always must be covered by liquid. If it isn't, pour in brine made of 2 tablespoons salt per 4¼ cups of water). After 10 days, the pre-fermentation phase is finished. Then, place the stoneware pot in a cool place such as a basement. After 8 weeks, the sauerkraut is ready. To ensure that the lid stays tightly sealed, now and then top up the water in the rim.

Sweet-and-Sour Pumpkin Pickle

This is a recipe from my friend Friederike. Every fall, she pickles pumpkins grown in her garden following this old family recipe. As a child, she didn't even want to taste pickled pumpkin, now she absolutely loves it. Linn

Makes about 8 jars 8oz (250ml) each

1 large pumpkin (about 4½lb (2kg))
3 cups white wine vinegar
2.2lb (1kg) sugar
10 cloves
1 piece of fresh ginger to taste

Cut the pumpkin in half, peel it, scrape out the seeds with a spoon, and chop the pumpkin flesh into cubes about ½in (1cm) in size. Place the pumpkin cubes in a large bowl, and add 2 cups of vinegar and 4¼ cups of water. Let the pumpkin marinate, uncovered, over night.

The next day, set a sieve over a large bowl to catch the liquid and pour the cubes of pumpkin into the sieve. Peel the ginger and either dice it finely or slice it finely into strips. Heat the marinade in a pot and add the remaining 1 cup of vinegar, the sugar, cloves, and ginger. Working in batches, boil the pumpkin in the liquid for about 5 minutes until it is soft. Using a slotted spoon, remove the pumpkin from the pot and fill them into sterilized jars. Fill a boiling-water canner half-full with water and heat the water until it is hot but not boiling.

Once all the pumpkin cubes are filled into the jars, ladle enough piping-hot cooking liquid into each jar so that the pumpkin is covered completely leaving ¼in (5mm) headspace. Seal the jars with sterilized self-sealing lids and jar rings, or rubber seals for hinged jars. Place the jars in the boiling-water canner, adding boiling water if needed to ensure the tops of the jars are covered by about 1in (2.5cm) of water. Over high heat, bring the water to a rolling boil and boil for 5 minutes. Stored in a cool, dark, place, the pickled pumpkin will keep for about 6 months.

Sweet-and-Sour Dill Pickles

Small, fresh, pickling cucumbers are only available for a few weeks of the year, from about July to mid September. These sweet-and-sour pickles are pickled in the traditional way with vinegar, sugar, and spices.

Makes 1 quart (1l)

1lb 2oz (500g) pickling cucumbers

1 onion

1 tbsp coarsely chopped dill (no stems)

10 mustard seeds

5 black peppercorns

⅓ cup white wine vinegar

4 tbsp sugar

2 tbsp salt

Thoroughly wash the cucumbers. Cut them into large pieces if they don't fit in the jar. Peel and finely dice the onion. Place the diced onion, dill, mustard seeds, peppercorns, and pickling cucumbers in a glass canning jar that you have just sterilized. Combine the white wine vinegar, 1¾ cups of water, sugar, and salt in a pot and heat until the sugar has dissolved. Fill the canning jar with the hot liquid leaving ½in (13mm) headspace. Cover the jar with a sterilized self-sealing lid and jar ring. Fill a boiling-water canner half-full with water and heat it until it is hot but not boiling. Place the jar in the boiling-water canner, adding boiling water if needed to ensure the jar is covered by about 1in (2.5cm) of water. Bring the water to a rolling boil over high heat and boil for 15 minutes. Let the jar of cucumbers cool for about 5 minutes before taking it out of the canner. Store the jar in a cool, dark, place. Let the pickles marinate for at least 14 days before opening.

TIP To make more jars, multiply the quantities accordingly. Another gentler method of canning the cucumbers is to place the jar(s) in a canner half-filled with warm water (140°F/60°C). Add enough hot water so that the jars are submerged in 1in (2.5cm) of water. Heat the water so that it boils between 356– 365 °F (180– 185 °C) for 30 minutes.

VARIATION Spreewald pickles: To make a stoneware pot that holds 5 quarts of pickles, you will need 6½lb (3kg) of pickling cucumbers, [...] picking cucumbers and pat them dry. Wash and coarsely chop the dill and savory, including the stems, and mix the herbs together. Dissolve the salt in 10½ cups of cold water to make a brine. Layer the bottom of the pot with half the dill and savory mixture, place a layer of cucumbers on top, and spread the other half of the herbs over them. Pour in the brine. Set a plate or a wooden board directly on the cucumbers so that they stay submerged in the brine. Marinate them at room temperature for 8–10 days. Then, they are ready to eat and will keep if stored in a cool place for about 3 weeks.

The Good Provisioner

Using leftovers creatively

What to do with bread dumplings left over from Sunday dinner? Or the leftover meat, the small bowls of pasta, mashed potatoes, or vegetables? Our grandmothers still knew how to be economical in a clever way so that as little as possible was wasted. And most of them were able to create new meals out of the previous day's leftovers, such as these:

Bread-dumpling salad: Turn leftover bread dumplings into dumpling salad, a tasty, cold, evening meal. Thinly slice the bread dumplings, some cooked sausage, and red radishes, and pour a dressing of vinegar, oil, salt, and pepper over the salad. A beer goes well with this typical Bavarian leftover meal.

Sweet pasta: Chop the leftover pasta a bit. Sweat a few tablespoons of bread crumbs in a generous amount of butter and lightly brown them. Add the pasta, mix well, and heat it up gently. Season to taste with sugar and a pinch of salt. Serve apricot spread or plum butter on the side.

Snow dumplings: A good way of using leftover egg whites is to beat 2 egg whites to the soft-peak stage, gradually add 2 tablespoons of sugar and beat until stiff peaks are formed. In a pot, heat up enough milk so the dumplings float in it. Moisten 2 teaspoons. Scoop small dumplings from the beaten egg whites and slide them into hot, but not boiling, milk. Cover, and poach them gently for 5 minutes. They go very well with fruit compote or cold fruit soup.

Egg liquor: A good use for leftover egg yolks is to beat together 6 large egg yolks with 1 cup confectioner's sugar and ¼ teaspoon pure vanilla extract. Add 5fl oz (150ml) vodka, white rum, or cognac, ¾ cup heavy cream, and 1¾ cups condensed milk. Slowly and thoroughly mix everything together. Fill the liquor into a sterilized wine bottle. Keep the liquor in the refrigerator and use it within 1–2 weeks. It tastes delicious with ice cream and fruit salad.

Chopped egg salad: When you have a number of hard-boiled eggs left over, such as after Easter, it's egg salad time. Finely chop the eggs and add a few chopped gherkins or capers. Add salt, pepper, chives, and a bit of mayonnaise and combine thoroughly. Spread a thick layer of egg salad on fresh whole-grain bread.

Potato cakes: Take leftover potatoes, mash them in a bowl, add 1–2 eggs, a bit of flour, salt, pepper, and nutmeg, and combine to form a firm dough. Let the dough rest for 30 minutes. Flour your hands and shape the dough into little potato cakes. Fry the cakes in hot oil until they are brown. Finely diced leftover ham, peas, or herbs (or all these together) also taste good added to the potato dough. Serve a tomato salad on the side.

Potato nests: Mix leftover mashed potatoes with 1–2 eggs, salt, and a bit of nutmeg. Depending on the consistency, mix in a bit more flour until the dough is pliable enough to pipe through a pastry bag. Line a baking tray with parchment paper. On the paper, pipe the small round bases first, then create the sides to form potato nests. Brush the nests with egg yolk and bake at 350°F (180°C) in a preheated oven until they are golden-brown. These nests are ideal filled with leftover warmed-up meat or vegetables.

Roasted meat salad: Leftover roast is quickly turned into a savory meat salad. Finely dice the meat and place it in a bowl along with gherkins, finely chopped onion, and flat-leaf parsley. Make a salad dressing using vinegar, oil, mustard, a bit of tomato paste, salt, pepper, and sugar. Pour it over the leftover roast, mix everything together well and let the salad marinate for at least 1 hour.

Vegetable timbale: This is a great way of using leftover vegetables such as cauliflower, Brussel sprouts, peas, and carrots, or kohlrabi—or also mixed vegetables. But you do need a steamed pudding mold with a lid. Mix about 1lb 10oz (750g) leftover vegetables with 3–4 beaten large eggs, chopped chives or flat-leaf parsley, grated cheese, a dash of heavy cream, dash of nutmeg, and salt to form a thick mixture. Grease a pudding mold and sprinkle it with bread crumbs. Pour the vegetable mixture up to three-quarters high, place the pudding mold in a water bath, and cook it for about 45 minutes.

Free and delicious

Whether it was wild herbs, blossoms, mushrooms, or fruit—it was once considered normal to gather Mother Nature's bounty. Today, too, it is a source of pride to prepare food that one has gathered oneself during a walk, and it's also fun.

Bear's-garlic butter: In spring, bear's garlic (*allium ursinum*), also known as wild garlic or ramsons, grows along woodland edges and even in parks. You can recognize it from afar by its garlic-like aroma. But be careful: the highly-toxic leaves of lily-of-the valley look almost identical! If you are not absolutely sure, do not pick the leaves. To make bear's-garlic butter, finely chop 1 handful of bear's-garlic leaves. Mix them with 4½oz (125g) softened butter and a pinch of salt. Shape the butter into a roll and wrap it in parchment paper. Put it in the refrigerator to harden. Serve bear's garlic butter instead of herbed butter with steak and fish.

Chocolate fir tips: Cut off the new, bright-green, tips of spruce or fir twigs. Melt dark chocolate in a water bath. Using a teaspoon, quickly dip the spruce tips into the chocolate, covering them completely. Place the tips on parchment paper and let cool. They taste delicious eaten the same day. Afterward, their taste and consistency deteriorates but you can freeze the chocolate tips and nibble on them frozen.

Elderflower fritters: To make crispy elderflower blossom fritters, make a pancake batter out of flour, egg, salt, and a dash of beer. Clean the elderflower blossom clusters and dip them one after the other into the batter. Deep fry them in hot oil right away. Dust with confectioner's sugar.

Elderflower syrup: Cut about 25 elderflower blossom clusters with their stems and carefully shake them to remove any insects. In a large pot, bring 2.2lb (1kg) sugar and 8½ cups water to a boil and remove from the heat. Slice 4 organic lemons. Put the elderflower blossoms and lemon slices in the sugar water and let them steep in the syrup for 3 days. Filter the syrup. Stir in 1½oz (30g) of citric acid and fill into four 16-fl oz (500-ml) bottles. Top up with water and a bit of lemon juice and serve the syrup as a thirst-quencher or as an aperitif with ice-cold sparkling wine.

Wild herb salad: Wash two handfuls each of young dandelion and nettle leaves, a bit of sorrel or bear's garlic leaves (see above), and a few daisy blossoms. Drain the leaves in a colander. Make a salad dressing with 3 tablespoons of lemon juice, 1 tablespoon of honey, salt, pepper, 1 small, grated onion, and 3 tablespoons of walnut oil (or olive oil). Toss the salad and serve immediately. Place one peeled, hot, soft-boiled egg on top of each plate of salad. If you would like a milder-tasting salad, mix in some Boston lettuce.

Treasures from the pantry

Skillful provisioning was once considered very important. Serving healthy and varied meals, even in winter, meant laying down fruit and vegetables and herbs during the harvest season. Today we can buy everything in the supermarket at any time. But it is still a great feeling when the basement and pantry are filled with harvest bounty.

Apples: Apples produce a gas that cause other types of fruit and vegetables to soften or spoil more quickly. For this reason, they should always be stored separately. Using thick layers of newspaper, line the bottoms of flat crates or drawers from an old chest-of-drawers, lay out the apples in them, and store them in the basement or garden shed. Check them often. Remove fruit showing brown spots immediately and use them.

Cucumbers & tomatoes: Never store cucumbers and tomatoes together, since they will both spoil more quickly. Store the cucumbers in the vegetable drawer of the refrigerator and eat them soon after picking. Small cucumbers can be pickled (*see* page 184). Do not store tomatoes in the refrigerator because they will lose their aroma. It is better to place them in rows on newspapers in an unheated room. Green tomatoes will ripen when stored in this way.

Herbs: Simply air-dry herbs. Especially good for air-drying are rosemary, sage, mint, thyme, bay leaf, and oregano which retain their flavor even after drying. Using thread or string, bind the herbs into small bundles and hang them from their stems, leaves down, in an airy, dry, place. As soon as they are dried, pluck the leaves from the stems and store them in containers with tight-fitting lids. Parsley, chives, dill, basil, and chervil lose flavor when they are dried, so always use them when they are fresh. (If you have large quantities of these herbs, chop them finely and freeze them in small portions.)

Lettuce & radishes: Cut a cross into the bottom of the head of lettuce and place it in a bowl of water; place radishes in a glass of water with the leaves down. Both will stay fresh and crisp.

Root vegetables: Carrots, red beets, and radishes belong in the sandbox. Yes, you read this correctly. After the harvest, remove the greens and layer the unwashed vegetables in sand. Buried in sand, they will keep for months in a cool basement. The sand should be kept a bit moist, but never wet.

Onions & garlic: These will remain fresh for a long time in a unglazed stoneware pot covered by a lid with holes in it; keep the pot in a dark, cool, place. Instead of a lid, you can also use a cotton or linen cloth and use a thick elastic band to secure it over the pot.

The Good Provisioner

Grandma's best secrets

Over-salted sauces, burned-on food, egg whites that don't form stiff peaks? These things happen and are no reason to throw down your spoon. By following Grandma's tried-and-true secrets, you can quickly rectify some common kitchen mishaps.

Lumpy bechamel sauce: Pour the sauce through a fine-meshed sieve into a clean pot. Press down on the lumps of flour with the back of a spoon and press them through the sieve. Boil the sauce again.

Over-salted gravy: Cut a raw potato into thick slices and add them to the gravy to cook along with the sauce for 10–15 minutes. Discard the potatoes.

The egg whites won't form stiff peaks: Add 1 pinch of salt and/or a few drops of lemon juice—this often helps. But to prevent this from happening in the first place, make sure you separate the eggs cleanly. Even the smallest trace of egg yolk will prevent egg whites from stiffening. Chill the egg whites and mixing bowl before using them. And beat the egg whites until they are almost stiff before adding the sugar.

Curdled hollandaise sauce: Quickly add an ice cube (or a bit of ice-cold water) and continue beating vigorously.

Over-salted clear broth: Lightly beat 2 egg whites and add them to the boiling broth. After a few minutes, remove the egg white with a slotted spoon.

The cake won't come out of the cake pan: Place the cake pan briefly in hot water. Or, wrap a moistened dish cloth around the pan for 1 minute.

Curdled mayonnaise: Beat 1 egg yolk with a bit of salt, and beat in the curdled mayonnaise in drops, then in a thin stream. To prevent this from happening at all, the egg yolk and oil have to be at room temperature. Adding 1 teaspoon of mustard or a few squeezes of lemon juice and 1 pinch of salt help prevent the mayonnaise from becoming runny.

The bread dumplings are not firm or are too firm: If they are not firm, add bread crumbs to the dumpling dough and let it swell up a bit. If they are too firm, boil them at a rolling boil, but keep the pot covered. Now and then, pour in a soup ladle of cold water.

The pot is burned: Place 1 teaspoon of baking powder in the pot, pour in some cold water (to about 2in/5cm high), bring the water to a rolling boil and boil it for a few minutes. Turn off the heat but let the pot stand for a bit. Then, clean off the black crust with a scouring sponge.

Index

INDEX OF GERMAN RECIPE TITLES

THE AUTHORS

Linn Schmidt loves poking around in flea-markets, attics, and old cookbooks looking for treasures and always wanted to write down all of her aunt's favorite recipes. An author and photographer, Linn is currently working as an editor. She lives in Hamburg with her family.

Birgit Hamm devours cookbooks like other people devour mystery novels. She was a cook in a trendy Frankfurt restaurant and the managing editor of a restaurant guide. Today Birgit works as an author and journalist and lives with her husband in Hamburg, where they both cook for friends at every opportunity.

Thanks to:

Ute and Marina for the studio; Astrid von Gustavia and Bridget Bell Hamburg for the dishes; Sabine and Annette for the pickles and green beans; Katharina, Tiffany, and Martin for cooking; Wilfried for the present; Sabine and Randy for the books; Berit and Gönke for the kitchen equipment; Constanze for the ideas; Jens of Restaurant Nil for the napkin; Christine Clausing of Hotel zur Bleiche for the tip; Oliver Heilmeyer of Restaurant 17fuffzig for the props; Florian Bucher for the text on page 121 and 123; Monika Schlitzer and Elke Homburg for their confidence in us; our families for their patience and support and, of course, our six main leading ladies for their participation.

DORLING KINDERSLEY
London, New York, Melbourne, Munich and Delhi

For DK, New York
Senior Editor Rebecca Warren
Editorial Director Nancy Ellwood

Text Birgit Hamm and Linn Schmidt
(text pp. 121 and 123 Florian Bucher)
Translation Barbara Hopkinson, Toronto
Photographs Linn Schmidt. Exceptions: p. 4
(Karina Mühlfarth), pp. 22–24, 56, 64, 76, 96,
174–177, 186 (Birgit Hamm), p. 23, 2nd. from
right (instamatics/iStockphoto), p. 52, opener
(dreadlock/Fotolia.com) and below center
(camera-me/Fotolia.com), p. 53, below right
(Jochen Hank/iStockphoto), pp. 120–123
(Barbara Bucher), p. 174, opener
(Ina Peters/iStockphoto)
Food Styling Birgit Hamm and Linn Schmidt,
Hamburg
Editor Claudia Krader, Munich
Graphic Design Catherine Avak, Munich
Repro Repro Ludwig Prepress & Multimedia
GmbH, Zell am See

For Dorling Kindersley Verlag, Munich
Publishing Manager Monika Schlitzer
Managing Editor Elke Homburg
Production Manager Dorothee Whittaker

First published under the title: Heimwehküche

© Dorling Kindersley Verlag GmbH, Munich,
first edition 2010 First American Edition, 2012

Published in the United States by
DK Publishing
375 Hudson Street
New York, New York 10014

14 13 12   10 9 8 7 6 5 4 3 2

003—184111—Sept/12

Copyright © 2012 Dorling Kindersley Limited
All rights reserved

Without limiting the rights under copyright reserved above, no part of this publication may be reproduced, stored in or introduced into a retrieval system, or transmitted, in any form, or by any means (electronic, mechanical, photocopying, recording, or otherwise), without the prior written permission of both the copyright owner and the above publisher of this book.

A catalog record for this book is available from the Library of Congress.
ISBN 978-0-7566-9432-6

DK books are available at special discounts when purchased in bulk for sales promotions, premiums, fund-raising, or educational use. For details, contact: DK Publishing Special Markets, 375 Hudson Street, New York, New York 10014 or SpecialSales@dk.com.

Printed and bound in China by
Leo Paper Products

Discover more at www.dk.com

My Recipes

My Recipes

My Recipes

My Recipes

My Recipes